Heidi is one of our heroes. We had the privilege of being there when God touched her powerfully and gave her nations. Since that time she has passionately pursued both her relationship with heaven and her mission from heaven. Her life story will transform yours.

—JOHN AND CAROL ARNOTT
Founding Pastors, Catch the Fire

Heidi has provoked, comforted, and inspired me with her life, message, and friendship. Her latest book, *Birthing the Miraculous*, is engaging, personal, and empowering. It awakened old dreams. It infused me with fresh hope. It also provoked me to a fresh surrender and abandonment in my obedience to the lover of my soul, Yeshua!

This book has the rawness, personal struggle, yet God-encouragement of the Book of Psalms. It also has the practical, fear-of-the-Lord-based wisdom of the Book of Proverbs. I highly recommend this book to a generation of world-changers, both young and old. It will inspire you to dream, take risks, and stay the course until the fullness of God's purposes are fulfilled in your life. This book will empower young leaders to start out their calling and journey with the right perspective and expectations, which will save them from years of disappointment and frustration. It will also encourage the more mature readers to launch out again with fresh-love-motivated, faith-fueled exploits no matter the cost.

God's call on my life to reach out to the Jewish people and Israel came at a time that I thought my life's calling was set and secure. This shook up my comfort zone theologically and my ministry focus and reputation. Heidi's book has encouraged me   :p leading us beyond ourselves and our natural understanding and ability. I, for one, will follow Heidi's challenge to carry God's promises to full term!

—Tod McDowell
Executive Director, Caleb Company
www.calebcompany.org

I heard Heidi preach a powerful message once called "Eat Slowly." She was addressing the subject of partaking deeply of the Lord's rich presence and Word without being in a hurry. When I read *Birthing the Miraculous*, I desired everyone to read it and to "eat it slowly," digesting every nugget and allowing the profound, Spirit-filled message to become flesh in them. I encourage you to read the book—eat slowly—then go and be the message. After all, you are what you eat!

—Patricia King
President, XPministries
www.xpmedia.com

I personally know of no other person living who reflects the attitude of Mary as depicted in this book more than Heidi Baker. She is one of the few people who could write such a book. *Birthing the Miraculous* is an amazing book full of stories that illustrate the principles Heidi so powerfully draws to our attention—an amazing book by an amazing missionary, a highly respected scholar with her PhD who not only knows how to properly interpret the Word of God but is also knowledgeable from experience of the truths she writes about.

This is a faith-building book. This is a practical book explaining the way to intimacy with God. This is a book for people who love missions. This is a book for people who love the presence of God. This is a book for people who love to learn about the power of God to work miracles and healings.

I want to encourage you to make this book a part of your library and read it more than once. I have personally witnessed the great move of God that is written about in this book. I have met the dead who were raised in Mozambique through Rolland and Heidi's ministry. I have seen personally the ears of the deaf open when she prayed for every deaf person at a meeting one night. I have seen blind eyes open on their base during a normal worship service on Sunday morning. I know it was not Heidi who raised the dead, opened the eyes of the blind, caused the deaf to hear—I know it was God. But I am so glad I can count her as my friend who is such a friend of Jesus, who out of her intimate relationship with Jesus has the privilege of co-laboring with Him and speaking commands on His behalf because she hears from Him what He wants to do. Read the book and then come to Mozambique to help answer not the Macedonian cry but the Mozambican cry.

—RANDY CLARK
Founder and President, Global Awakening
and the Apostolic Network of Global Awakening

How can it be that the life of one simple village girl from a very small town called Nazareth has impacted billions of people for the better throughout the ages? This book reveals in a clear and powerful way the attitude, heart, and principles that make it possible for Mary to be used by God in such a wonderful way.

How can it be that a young girl from Laguna Beach followed the footsteps of Mary when hearing from God, seeking Him with all her heart, daring to believe what He told her, and then loving Him with an undying passion? Heidi Baker has sacrificed everything to serve Him in the poorest and the most challenging places on earth, resulting in tens of thousands of abandoned and neglected children being loved and taken care of in all the Iris centers worldwide.

I have been privileged to call Heidi and her wonderful, Jesus-loving husband, Rolland, our dearest friends for over thirty years. God has worked mightily in my own life and others', but I hold Heidi and Rolland with the highest esteem for their determination and dedication to love and serve the millions who are "the least of these" in our world.

I trust that this book will inspire and encourage the readers to allow the Holy Spirit to fill them with His grace and calling so that they too will make a difference in the lives of multitudes in their own spheres of influence in this generation for the glory of God!

—MEL TARI
Author, *Like a Mighty Wind*

I remember being at a service where Heidi Baker began to share about the reality of carrying the promise. She invited us all to glimpse into the life of Mary, the mother of Jesus. Her message marked me in a profound way.

As I read the pages of this book, it is as if I can hear Heidi speak again words of truth, humility, endurance, and promise. I began to read the hard questions: What was it like for this young girl to say yes and to carry the promise of God within her? How did Mary carry on in life with the daily scrutiny of everyone's eyes as they watched the promise begin to grow on the inside of her small frame? Heidi has such a gift of communication, writing simply in a way a child would understand and yet, in the same sentence, revealing profound truths that a theologian would need to ponder.

With each chapter I am reminded again that my little yes counts. My little life counts before God. This book is a timely message of a life laid down for her beloved King, inviting the world to do the same.

—Julie Meyer
Worship Leader, International House of Prayer

I'll never forget the night I sat on a rubber boat with Heidi Baker, pulling up to what was an unreached village shoreline with only the light of the moon leading the way. The cries of children could be heard in the distance—children who had just come to know Jesus in the past few years because of the sacrifice Heidi and Rolland had made to reach them with God's love. This one village who had never known Jesus was now 100 percent Spirit-filled believers.

I was overwhelmed by what I witnessed. The image of this little blonde lady sitting in the dirt holding children, reading Bible passages, singing worship songs, and praying for the sick, all by moonlight, deeply impacted me.

The anointing is a free gift from God, but pouring that anointing out has a price. Ministry has a price. Fulfilling God's call is not always easy, nor is it convenient. In the pages of this book you will read the riveting story of a woman and her family and the price that was paid to answer and fulfill the call of God. I have been to Mozambique, Africa, with Heidi and Rolland Baker. I have seen their lives firsthand. I have seen the sacrifice and at times the deep pain that accompany fulfilling a call from God. I have also seen the glorious fruit and magnificence of God's glory amidst the suffering and price being paid.

Your heart and perspective on answering God's call and seeing that call fully birthed into manifestation will be transformed by the inspiring testimonies of a woman who has laid her life down for Jesus and His children. You will learn the reality of what it takes to not only carry God's heart and vision, but also to birth that vision into reality. You will learn the joy of obedience and discover not only how to receive a vision from God but also how to give birth to it and nurture it to maturity.

I highly recommend this book for all who would dare to truly discover what it means to walk out a call and destiny in God. Heidi and Rolland Baker have become heroes in the faith to me. I love them with all my heart, and I know your life will be transformed with each page of this book.

—MATT SORGER
Author and TV Host, *Power for Life*
www.mattsorger.com

BIRTHING
the
MIRACULOUS

BIRTHING
the
MIRACULOUS

HEIDI BAKER

CHARISMA
HOUSE

Most CHARISMA HOUSE BOOK GROUP products are available at special quantity discounts for bulk purchase for sales promotions, premiums, fund-raising, and educational needs. For details, write Charisma House Book Group, 600 Rinehart Road, Lake Mary, Florida 32746, or telephone (407) 333-0600.

BIRTHING THE MIRACULOUS by Heidi Baker
Published by Charisma House
Charisma Media/Charisma House Book Group
600 Rinehart Road
Lake Mary, Florida 32746
www.charismahouse.com

Unless otherwise noted, all Scripture quotations are from the Holy Bible, New International Version. Copyright © 1973, 1978, 1984, International Bible Society. Used by permission.

Scripture quotations marked ESV are from the Holy Bible, English Standard Version. Copyright © 2001 by Crossway Bibles, a division of Good News Publishers. Used by permission.

Cover design by Justin Evans
Design Director: Bill Johnson

Visit the author's website at www.irisglobal.org.

Library of Congress Cataloging-in-Publication Data:

Baker, Heidi.

  Birthing the miraculous : the power of personal encounters
with God to change your life and the world / Heidi Baker.

    pages cm

  Summary: "God has promised us miracles. Are you willing
to do what it takes to see them through? In Birthing the
Miraculous, best-selling author Heidi Baker weaves true
stories from her life and ministry together with the biblical
story of Mary's pregnancy with Jesus to show readers how
to carry the promises of God in their own lives and become
a catalyst for God's glory here on earth. Her personal
visitations and life-changing visions demonstrates how
encounters with God have an amazing power to transform
individual lives and societies"-- Provided by publisher.

  ISBN 978-1-62136-219-7 (paperback) -- ISBN 978-1-62136-
294-4 (e-book)

  1. Christian life. 2. Miracles. 3. Immaculate Conception.
4. Mary, Blessed Virgin, Saint. I. Title.

  BV4509.5.B355 2014
  231.7--dc23

                                        2013038284

Some names have been changed to protect parties
ministering in dangerous locations.

While the author has made every effort to provide accurate
telephone numbers and Internet addresses at the time of
publication, neither the publisher nor the author assumes
any responsibility for errors or for changes that occur after
publication.

This publication is translated in Spanish under the title *El
nacimiento de lo milagroso*, copyright © 2014 by Heidi Baker,

published by Casa Creación, a Charisma Media company.
All rights reserved.

16 17 18 19 20 — 11 10 9 8 7

Printed in the United States of America

I dedicate this book to my amazing family:
Rolland, my husband, who is a very patient and
courageous man; Crystalyn, our daughter, who
is carrying her own glorious promises, along
with her husband, Brock Human, whom God
picked out just for her; and Elisha, our brilliant
son, who is spiritually one of the deepest
Christians I know and was a tremendous help
and editor for this book. I want to thank a
precious spiritual daughter, Dr. Jen Miskov,
for her editing and for being an inspiration
to me. And a special thanks goes to Laura
Taranto, one of our amazing laid-down-lover
ministers in Mozambique, who stayed up with
me night after night with power outages and
the Internet down, fueled by chocolate and the
Holy Spirit during the final hours of our third
final deadline with one minute until midnight.

This book is also dedicated to all the loyal, laid-
down, holy-given lovers of God who serve in
our Iris Global family in over thirty countries
around the world. And finally Ania, one of my
best friends, who has carried this labor of love
with me to bring forth the promise of this book.

CONTENTS

FOREWORD

BIRTHING THE MIRACULOUS is a book that few people could write—or at least write well. For such a book to be outstanding, the author would need to draw from a supernatural lifestyle that is rare not just in modern times but also in all of church history. In the case of this author that lifestyle is a miracle realm of biblical proportion. I have seen it firsthand.

My friendship with Rolland and Heidi Baker goes back about sixteen years. I have watched as these sold-out lovers of God have stepped into realms of breakthrough that few have even dreamed of. I will never forget one of my visits to Mozambique, when two blind men found their way to the Iris Global compound in the city of Pemba. After we had prayed over them for a short while, I heard Heidi tell them, "Come back tomorrow, and you will see!" The following day was a Sunday.

As the new day dawned, the activity level of their base increased dramatically as many from the community began to gather to celebrate God's goodness in their Sunday morning worship service. The worship of this body of believers was passionate and almost timeless. It was anything but a ritual or a token of their affection for God.

The blind men came back as they were instructed. What made their condition unique to me was that one of them only had white eyes. There was no pupil, iris, or anything. After a very brief time of prayer, both of these men could see. And the one with white eyes had brand-new, beautiful brown eyes. They both joyfully came to faith in Jesus that day and joined in the procession of new believers across the street to the ocean, where they would all be baptized. It was beautiful. It was perfect.

Because the Bakers live in such a desperate part of the world and because they look for the most difficult cases through which to display the love of God, they experience more than their share of tragedy and sorrow. I know of no one who has faced greater challenges to their faith than Rolland and Heidi Baker. Yet joy reigns supreme. I have watched as the gut-wrenching losses have been surpassed by the overwhelming encounters and breakthroughs that can come only from God's goodness.

I mention this because it is important for the reader to know that this book did not emerge out of a good meeting or one positive experience. Neither did its formation come from a classroom of theorists. It has been forged in the fires of adversity with many tears. Yet out of it all, we see the gospel of the kingdom come forth with the beauty and power spoken of in the Scriptures. And in case you might think this is only for uniquely gifted people, it is the army of children cared for by the Bakers' ministry that are some of the best at bringing a miracle to an impossible situation.

With this background, you might better appreciate how

Heidi is able to give the priceless insights and valuable keys to living out God's promises for your life. This book will bring encouragement and wisdom wherever you are in your journey. Through the story of her own life, she shows the importance of holding a promise that God has given you until it comes to completion.

I have felt for years that Mary, the mother of Jesus, would provide unusual glimpses into the last-days lifestyle of bringing forth the miracle to this world. Heidi does just that—brilliantly. She looks closely at how Mary managed her heart and life in the midst of many challenging circumstances.

Whether, like Mary, you are at the stage of receiving a promise from God that seems impossible, are navigating reactions from those around you, or are seeking wisdom for something never seen before, this book will draw you closer to the Father and give you great tools for thriving in the journey.

Heidi highlights the central key of keeping intimacy at the center of your journey and invites readers into being laid down, surrendered, and lost in love with God. She shows that this is how to be fearless and find hope and perseverance in the hardest moments. I have watched her and Rolland live this way for years and am convinced this is at the heart of their success in God.

The Lord told Heidi, "Only when you work together will you bring in the harvest." Heidi explains the joy and strength of partnering with the body of Christ in seeing promises fulfilled, and she shares her vision for seeing the next generation raised up and running in their destiny, carrying promises that go beyond one generation to see a multiplication of God's love in the world.

This book will inspire, encourage, and provide great clarity for this next season in God.

—BILL JOHNSON
Senior Pastor, Bethel Church, Redding, CA
Author, *When Heaven Invades Earth*
and *Hosting the Presence*

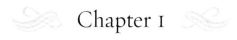

Chapter 1

TAKE HOLD *of the* PROMISE

In the sixth month, God sent the angel Gabriel to Nazareth, a town in Galilee, to a virgin pledged to be married to a man named Joseph, a descendant of David. The virgin's name was Mary. The angel went to her and said, "Greetings, you who are highly favored! The Lord is with you." Mary was greatly troubled at his words and wondered what kind of greeting this might be. But the angel said to her, "Do not be afraid, Mary, you have found favor with God. You will be with child and give birth to a son, and you are to give him the name Jesus. He will be great and will be called the Son of the Most High. The Lord God will give him the throne of his father David, and he will reign over the house of Jacob forever; his kingdom will never end."

—LUKE 1:26–33

I LIVE IN NORTHERN Mozambique. I spend some part of each week visiting backcountry villages. I am familiar with simple village life in places without power, running water, or large amounts of contact with the outside world. I often think Mary must have been from a place not so different from these little African communities. I wonder what she was doing when the angel appeared to her. I imagine her busy with ordinary tasks—fetching water from the well, washing her clothes in a clay pot, frying fish over a wood fire.

On that day I don't think she expected the angelic encounter that would overturn her world. What would your reaction be if an angel appeared to tell you that you were "highly favored"?

I have seen angels. I have felt the Lord's presence fall on a room like a heavy weight and drive everyone to their knees. I think most of us would fall on our faces in awe and terror. We would tremble before a holy God.

Mary's response was like this. She was more than a little bit concerned. She was terrified. The Bible tells us she was "greatly troubled." Personally I do not think it likely that she was already stunningly able or spectacular in her spiritual life. She was probably an ordinary teenage girl who loved God simply. I imagine she was much like any one of us—a little jar of clay.

What young girl would know how to respond when an angel showed up in her room to tell her she would become pregnant by the favor of God? What would she do? How would she tell her parents? "Mom, rejoice with me! An angel came, and now I'm pregnant! Everybody, let's have a party!"

What about her fiancé? Would she say, "Joseph, I cannot wait to tell you the news! I am so excited! God has found favor with me—and I am going to have a baby! It is not yours, but do not worry. It is a wonderful gift. Be happy with me, Joseph!"

We all think we want a word from God, but would we

want to receive one like this? Many of us want miracles in our lives. Mary's example teaches us that sometimes the most spectacular miracles will get us into equally spectacular trouble. Mary's gift had harsh consequences. She could hide it for only so long. Eventually her promise started to show, and she had to give an account for it. I wonder how many believed her when she told them she was pregnant because the Holy Spirit had overshadowed her.

Sometimes God's promises will look like this: bizarre, implausible, and even crazy. At times great promises will invite misunderstanding from those around us—even to the point of reproach.

What Kind of Favor Is This?

If we desire the favor of God on our lives, we should consider what it might look like. It is not always going to be cash and promotions and the like. Mary's favor was that of a simple Jewish girl who suddenly found herself pregnant. In all likelihood she would have had to deal with terrible gossip, criticism, and disapproval from her community. The first thing she had to do was nurture, protect, and love the life growing within her despite a great deal of misunderstanding and pain.

If God speaks to us in an unusual way, gives us a strange task, or tells us to go somewhere unexpected, we may be hesitant to tell our friends and family about it. We quite naturally worry about how people will react. Imagine for a moment how Mary felt when she had to tell her family about her visitation and about the wonderful promise from God now growing within her—not only that she was a virgin, but also that the child within her was the Son of God, Israel's Messiah.

Sometimes we wonder how we are going to explain far simpler things to people. Not everyone sees the wisdom in giving everything away before going to sit with the destitute in bombed-out third world streets. Not everyone understands forty-day fasts. Not everyone understands going to preach Jesus in places where you could be stoned for doing so. Not everyone understands giving your entire life to caring for victims of the sex-trade industry in India or submitting to the discipline of places such as Harvard and Yale for the gospel's sake.

The truth is that sometimes our family and friends will not understand the destiny we carry. Even if they do, it might come ten or twenty years after we have embraced it.

When I was sixteen years old, the Holy Spirit overshadowed me. The first thing that happened was that I lost all of my friends. When I told my family about the calling I had received, they were not sympathetic. They were convinced I was in a cult. Soon after that I had to give up a man I loved with all my heart. The Lord told me he was not my future husband.

A few years later I met the man I would marry, Rolland. When we eventually got married, we left immediately for the mission field. We had one-way tickets and thirty dollars to our name. Since then we have been ministering to the poor and the broken in Asia, England, and Africa, loving them into the kingdom one by one.

It was many years before my parents would even speak to me about what I was doing with my life. However, before they passed away, I had the incredible joy of leading them both to Jesus. My father went so far as to become an ordained minister at the age of seventy-two! When he passed away, my mother came to live with me in Mozambique for several months, teaching our children English and helping our ministry with great joy.

God restores all things!

"God Is Giving Me a City!"

When I was eighteen, I attended a meeting at Southern California College—now Vanguard University—that focused my life even more intensely.

I remember being flustered and upset with the speaker at this meeting because what he was saying seemed so arrogant. The only reason I kept listening was that I was part of the ministry team hosting him. I had to stay in the front row. But he said things that made no sense to me. They were too unbelievable, too awesome. The man stood there and said God had told him that He was giving him a city. He said it twice: "God told me He is giving me a city!"

As I was thinking how arrogant the man was, suddenly I saw two angels, one on his left and one on his right. Then, right behind him, I saw Jesus Himself. He was bright and shining.

It was an open vision. I was wide awake, still able to see all the ordinary things and people around me. Jesus pointed right at me and said, "Listen to him. He is telling the truth!"

I could not go to class after that. I crawled from that front row all the way to a little prayer room in the back of the chapel and worshipped God from the bottom of my soul all day. Weeping, I cried out to God that if it was true, I wanted Him to give me a nation.

It seemed to me that if God could give someone a city, He could also give someone a nation. That encounter changed me forever.

A Million-Dollar Conference

Almost twenty years later Randy Clark laid hands on me during a conference session at the Toronto Airport Christian Fellowship (now Catch the Fire) and said to me, "God wants to know—do you want the nation of Mozambique?"

My husband, Rolland, and I had gone to this revival in Canada because we were desperate and hungry for more of God. It was especially costly for us to attend because another large church had said if we returned to Toronto, we would lose their million-dollar pledge to build a new children's center for us. This particular church had severe theological objections to what was happening at Toronto. They didn't want to be associated with that movement in any way, even indirectly through us.

We needed the money desperately. We had recently lost close to all we had in Africa when local government officials had beaten up our children and taken away our first children's center and property in one weekend. Our family, staff, and three hundred twenty children had been left without homes.

This church wanted us to sign a letter promising we would never return to the revival churches at Toronto or Pensacola or else we could formally give up any expectation of receiving the money they had offered us.

Although we were in great need, this was not a difficult choice for us. We wanted more of the presence of

God at any cost. Even so we felt the price of coming to the next conference at Toronto deeply—it had a million-dollar entrance fee!

The pastor who withheld the money remained very precious to us, and we continue to honor his ministry. We were eventually reconciled to him, but at the time he simply did not understand many of the manifestations that happened in Toronto as people were touched by the Spirit of God.

At the conference Randy Clark preached with great fire and conviction about the anointing, power, and destiny God wants to release upon us. In the middle of his message, I suddenly began to feel such desperation for God that I could not hold myself back from responding. There was no altar call, not even a pause in his message, but in front of thousands of people, I felt compelled to run up to the altar. I knelt down there, lifted up my hands, and started screaming.

Even I wondered what I was doing. I could not believe I was acting so wildly. Naturally speaking, I would never behave that way, but the Holy Spirit had consumed me with so much longing for His presence that I no longer cared what anyone thought.

Randy stopped preaching. He put his hands on me and said, "God wants to know, do you want the nation of Mozambique?"

I screamed "Yes!" with everything within me.

He continued, "The blind will see, the deaf will hear, the crippled will walk, the dead will be raised, and the poor will hear the good news."

The power of God hit me like lightning. I vibrated and

screamed. I truly thought I was going to die. The impression I felt from God was, "Good. I want you dead."

I do believe God wants us to die—but He doesn't want to leave us dead. He wants us dead so we can be resurrected in the power of His glory. He wants to give us a new life that is no longer our own but given wholly to Him.

I remember a cry of "Yes!" that passed directly from my heart to His. I didn't think about it. If I had thought about it, I probably would have screamed "No!"

For seven days and seven nights after that, I felt the presence and power of God so intensely that I was disabled. I was unable to walk, talk, or move. The Holy Spirit had to tell people to pour water down my throat once in a while to give me a drink. I had to be carried to the restroom.

Many people laughed. The whole thing seemed funny to them. There was nothing funny about it to me. It was a powerful and holy time.

After this impartation we returned to Mozambique.

Over the next year our circumstances became more challenging than ever. Rolland and our daughter came down with multiple cases of severe malaria. I was diagnosed with multiple sclerosis. Our financial situation became even worse. Our Mozambican children were living in tents with worms and rats biting their toes at night.

I kept believing in the word given to me. During that whole year, I prayed for healing for all of the blind people I met in Mozambique. They all met Jesus, but none of them saw.

Then, after one year, God opened the heavens. The word started coming true. The blind began to see. The deaf began to hear. The crippled began to walk. Three of our Mozambican pastors raised people from the dead. Church growth exploded. Our history ever since has been filled to the brim with wild and wonderful tales.

At the time of this prophetic word we had planted one church in Hong Kong, one in England, and two in Mozambique. That was the visible fruit we had after many years of ministry. We had two small Mozambican churches—and that was with compulsory attendance at the children's center, where our children had to attend church before eating lunch on Sundays. Our other church met in a garbage dump.

Since that time our movement has seen more than ten thousand churches planted in and around Mozambique. Branches of the work have spread to more than thirty nations worldwide. A few thousand of these new churches are in Cabo Delgado Province in the far north of Mozambique, our adopted home and the home of the Makua and Makonde tribes—previously the largest unreached people groups in southeastern Africa.

When the Lord spoke to me about His desire for the entire nation of Mozambique to know Him, it felt bizarre for Him to ask me for help. We had experienced limited ministry success according to the world's standards. We had seen a few miracles, but by comparison this promise sounded too huge to contemplate. It seemed every bit as strange to me as God's word had probably seemed to Mary.

I know I am just one tiny person in the big picture of God's glorious purpose for Mozambique. I am one little mama ministering in the dirt. But I believe that if God can use a donkey, He can use me. I want to be a catalyst for God's glory. I want to believe God can cause His love and glory to shine out of my little laid-down life—and out of your little laid-down life. No matter how impossible a promise from God seems, we can respond as Mary did, with a yielded cry of "Yes!"

Even the smallest yes matters to God.

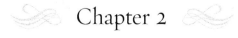

Chapter 2

JUST SAY YES!

> *And Mary said, "Behold, I am the servant of the Lord; let it be to me according to your word." And the angel departed from her.*
> —LUKE 1:38, ESV

SAYING YES TO the promises of God can be costly. Mary knew there would be a price. Personally I believe she could have said no. She might have said something like, "You are awesome. You are beautiful. But you are scaring me. Please. I am a virgin. I do not want this. Find someone else." She might have been overwhelmed by the prospect of shame, of ridicule, or perhaps of losing her betrothed.

Many of us ultimately respond to God's words with these kinds of fears. In the Lord's manifest presence we may be stirred with profound emotion and receive lofty promises, but what happens afterward?

Once the Holy Spirit overshadowed Mary, her life was permanently altered. There were lifelong difficulties she had to accept. And I believe the Lord still looks for those who will pay all it costs to carry His promises to fruition. He looks for a church, for a people, for worshippers who will not care about the reproach, who will not care about being stretched or pulled or inconvenienced, who will let the Lord take all of them.

Being pregnant comes with great weight, discomfort, and inconvenience. What will you do when carrying God's promise begins to strain you? Will you say, "Please, God, take away the promise! I can't do it anymore. It is too hard. I can't walk this walk. It is too heavy! Give my destiny to someone else."

Or will you yield, even in the midst of all the radical changes the promise brings—even as it stretches and pulls everything about you into a new shape?

People in the world sometimes abort their babies because they don't want to make the sacrifices children require. These sacrifices may seem like too great an incon-venience. The price seems too great. The church has some-times done the same thing with the promises, prophecies, and wooings of God. We have said yes in worship when we felt moved but then aborted what God asked us to carry when things started to feel difficult or inconvenient.

God does not like abortion! It breaks His heart because when we carry that which He placed inside us to full term, His lost sons and daughters—those He planned to reach through our laid-down lives—can come home. He loves to bring in people from darkness. He loves to bring in the lost and the dying and the sick and the broken.

The Lord is looking for those who are so in love with Him that they will say yes when they are wooed and still say yes when great sacrifice is required.

I believe Mary, as she was overshadowed by the Holy

Spirit, was engulfed in God's love and might have said to herself, "Though this will cause me incredible pain, though this will cause my reputation to be utterly ruined, though my fiancé may not understand, though my family may disown me, I will carry Your promise to full term, God. I will bear the reproach because I love You. I will carry whatever You place inside of me for love's sake."

What was Mary's response to a seemingly impossible promise? *Yieldedness.*

The Lord can use anyone who will respond to Him as Mary did—who says, "Be it unto me according to your word." He will use anyone who has a willing heart. And I believe that through intimacy with God, we can find a place of yielded love in which all fear disappears, a place in which we become willing to do anything and go anywhere for love's sake.

That place is the only reason I go where I go. I go for the sake of love. I am completely in love with God. I am undone by His love. I am simply someone who asked the Lord to let it be unto me according to His word. Every morning when I wake up, the first thing I ask is for the Holy Spirit to possess me. I pray it all the time. I want to be fully possessed. I do not know how to pray complicated things. I just say, "Possess me, Holy Spirit! Let me love like Jesus today. Let me be His fragrance. Let me be His life. Let me carry what You have placed within me this day. I love You, Holy Spirit. I love You, Jesus. I love You, Daddy God!"

Loving Jesus at Any Price

I have felt overshadowed by the Lord several times in my life. The first time was at the age of sixteen. I met Jesus on an Indian reservation in central Mississippi in a Baptist church. The next night I was baptized by the beautiful Holy Spirit at a Pentecostal Holiness church.

Five months later I was worshipping the One who is altogether worthy. The Holy Spirit came, and again I felt overshadowed by Him. During worship the brilliant light of God came, and I was taken up in a vision. I could no longer hear the sermon or anything else around me. This church was extraordinarily loud, but when I felt the Lord descend upon me, all of its many sounds went away. I froze, with my hands up in the air, and then I heard the audible voice of God for the first and only time in my life thus far.

It seemed that Jesus spoke to me, kissing the ring finger on my left hand while oil ran down my arm. I heard Him say, "You will be married to Me. You are called to be a minister and a missionary to Africa, Asia, and England."

I remained stuck in the same position for three whole hours, kneeling before the Lord without moving, lost in the vision.

That day I discovered a new part of my destiny.

After the overwhelmingly heavy presence of God lifted, I fell apart. I sobbed and I laughed. I have pursued that vision with everything within me for more than three decades since. I have not done anything else. I moved straight ahead as Jesus called me because He ruined me with His love. That visitation so impacted me that I told Jesus that I do not care what it costs.

I bore the reproach of membership in a Pentecostal Holiness church while living in Laguna Beach, California. For years I did not wear trousers or cut my hair because I thought it was not holy. I did not know at that time that I did not have to make those sacrifices to be holy—but that was what I was taught, so I made them. I was willing to carry the promise no matter what it cost me. Those precious, beautiful people at the Pentecostal Holiness church taught me to joyfully bear reproach for the gospel and to pay its cost. I am forever grateful that they taught me to love Jesus at any price.

When I felt the Lord overshadow me, He planted a promise inside of me. That day something began growing within me—a call and a ministry. Even though it took me nearly twenty years to get to Africa, the very next day after the vision I began to step out into my destiny.

When God called me to be a minister, I had never seen a woman preach. I did not know they could. I was baptized and confirmed in a formal church where there were no women ministers. I had never seen or heard of women ministering. But I had heard from the Lord that I was to minister, so the next day I started to speak to whomever would listen.

I did not wait for someone to invite me to speak in a church or conference. Back then no one invited sixteen-year-old girls to things like that, so I found Alzheimer's patients to minister to. They did not remember if I came, and they did not know when I left. They did not look at their watches. I could minister as long as I was led to do so.

I also ministered to drug addicts. I sat with them and shared the gospel while they were stoned out of their minds. I asked God to let me pour His love out on them. Even though I was told women did not preach, no one tried to tell me I could not love and speak to drug addicts.

I went into the darkness and carried the light God placed inside me. I looked for places where people were sad, broken, sick, dying, and desperate. I have been doing that for more than thirty-seven years now. Those are still my favorite kinds of places to be. I found out that the broken and dying are always hungry. They are always desperate. They know they are in need.

> Blessed are the poor in spirit, for theirs is the kingdom of heaven.
> —MATTHEW 5:3

Some of you may have carried prophetic words for years and yet have never stepped out into them because they seem too costly, too foolish, or too impossible. Maybe you do not feel you are prepared enough, or maybe you are afraid for anyone to know what you feel God said to you, because then you might actually be held responsible for acting on His words. Perhaps His promises come with such serious social stigma that you aren't sure you really want to carry them.

There may be a steep price for what God has placed inside you, but if you want Him, you will choose to pay it. You may have a whole bag of promises, but what are you going to do with them? Will you bear the possible reproach and carry to full term that which God put inside of you? It is easy to hear a great prophetic word but often costly and challenging to bring it to birth.

God has predestined every single one of us for fruitfulness. (See John 15.) We need to be familiar with a place of divine intimacy in which we are so consumed by the Holy Spirit that we will nurture and protect the seed He places in us. We need to fearlessly step out and activate His promises. It is intimacy that gives us the grace and strength we need to push through suffering, pain, and inconvenience.

When I got back to Laguna Beach after my encounter at the Indian reservation, I had the seed of God's promise inside of me. Every single friend I had—including my family—thought I was out of my mind. It seemed as if I had lost everyone close to me, but I pressed in for more of God's presence. I told Jesus that I would still trust Him and continue to receive His love and give it away.

God is looking for people who will welcome His presence to hover over them freely. When the Lord's presence hovers over you, there will be increasing fruitfulness in your life. It is inevitable. Fruit always follows intimacy, and God is calling us to exponential fruitfulness. He is calling us to be people who are absolutely enthralled by the beauty of Jesus—married to Him, in love with Him, desperate for Him, wooed by Him, set apart for Him, given wholly to Him, and laid down for Him in every area of our lives.

Chapter 3

The SECRET PLACE

> *As Moses went into the tent, the pillar of cloud would*
> *come down and stay at the entrance, while the LORD*
> *spoke with Moses.... The LORD would speak to Moses*
> *face to face, as man speaks with his friend.... The LORD*
> *replied, "My presence will go with you, and I will give*
> *you rest." Then Moses said to him, "If your Presence*
> *does not go with us, do not send us up from here."*
> —EXODUS 33:9, 11, 14–15

MOSES KNEW THE importance of dwelling in God's presence. He longed to spend time in the secret place. He hungered to be in God's presence so much that he would not move forward without Him. He told God, "How will anyone know that you are pleased with me and with your people unless you go with us?" (Exod. 33:16). Joshua also knew the importance of dwelling with God in the secret place. We find that when Moses returned to the Israelite camp after God had spoken to him "as a man speaks with his friend," Joshua did not leave the tent. He stayed in God's presence (v. 11).

We too must realize that developing a life in God's presence above all else is the only way to fulfill our God-given destinies. Keys to our callings are released when we spend time there. We must always run to Him in the secret place to find the true source of life.

What's more, when we spend time in the secret place, our passion and hunger for Jesus grow. It is only as we abide in His presence that the most precious treasures can be born. This is much better than work! More is accomplished by spending time in God's presence than by doing anything else.

There are no shortcuts to the anointing. If we want to fully walk out the callings the Lord places on our lives, we must spend time with Him, cultivating intimacy in the secret place.

The Secret to Sustainability

There is a time for wooing, and there is a time for work. It is important to know the difference. We all need to work. However, when God begins wooing us, it is important to recognize it's time to cease working and enter into His glorious presence.

I work very hard. I am a very responsible person. But there are moments when God draws me to Himself even closer and asks me to come away from all of the activity and spend time alone with Him. I have to respond. I have to drop everything else. I want to come so close to God that I am totally hidden in Him. I am continually hungry and thirsty for more of His Spirit. I have no appetite for anything else but Him. The only thing that truly satisfies me is being in His presence, and it is His wooing that brings me to a place of surrender. In holy surrender I find all the strength I need to run the race.

In fact, I don't know how to run the race without the wooing. Without romance I cannot be a minister. I have tried before—I just cannot do it. I do not even want to. But when I am in love, I will run eighteen hours a day. I will run after Him with everything inside of me, and I will be at rest, even as I am running.

In this life we can run ourselves to exhaustion doing more and more things for God without ever understanding what He really desires from us. God longs to increase our appetite for Himself. If we will eat and drink of Him, He will bring us into the relationship that will transform us into His likeness. We will begin to eat and drink of Jesus so deeply every day that we no longer grow weary or get exhausted as we run our race. We will learn to simply live in the secret place of His heart continually.

People often ask me what the secret to sustainability is. The secret place is the secret. We have to live there. As we abide in the presence of the Lord, our hunger increases, and we find ourselves birthing glorious new life. If you think you know how to live in the secret place but there is no fruit in your life, you have not been there. To the degree we are united with God's heart and in love with Jesus, we will be fruitful.

When I talk to my coworkers, I always emphasize this same thing. Over and over again I say, "All fruitfulness flows from intimacy." I always remind our team that intimacy is the only way to bear fruit that lasts.

When new ministers first get to Africa or Asia, some

of them think they understand this, but when the poor are banging on their door and need help, I watch the ones who listen, stopping often to spend time in the secret place, and I watch the ones who do not. The ones who do not listen work very hard for several months. I watch them work, move, push, and forget to stop each day to eat bread from heaven. Then I watch them get on planes and return to the Western world in exhaustion.

I watch those who have learned the mystery of the secret place too. They understand that when they seek more time with God, they will bear far more fruit and will have the grace to keep running, even in the midst of great pressure. They thrive over the years because they have learned to abide in the realm where we are all called to live.

The Secret to Divine Strategies

I have a confession to make. I have no idea how to prepare for conferences and meetings. I simply live in communion with God, where fruitfulness can flow. Preparing my life to overflow is the only way I know how to prepare.

Before we take any action in our movement, the Lord reveals His strategy to us. There is not one thing we are doing or attempting to do that we did not find in His Word and His presence. We did not sit down at a whiteboard and draw out plans for how we are going to reach the nations. Instead, God gave us a vision to care for a million children.

When the Lord first showed me the revival that would come to Mozambique, I had planned for our ministry to take in only a few hundred more children. I thought that was the best we could do because we did not have many fathers for them, only mothers and other young adults.

Not long afterward God gave us a fresh strategy to go with the vision. He spoke to us and said He was going to touch the hearts of the fathers to care for the children and bring them into their own homes.

We believed God, and now there is an extraordinary movement. From the communities where they have planted churches, many pastors are taking in children who need care. Most of these children are cared for in the homes of these pastors or by widows and others in those same communities.

We do not claim to have a perfect model. We make mistakes, but we are simply doing what God has given us to do and learning as we go. More and more children are being cared for every day as we seek God's heart for the nation of Mozambique and other nations, making every effort to remain constantly within His presence.

The truth is, we cannot step out and transform any place for God unless we carry what He calls us to carry. When we live in His presence, nations begin to change, one person at a time. Whether God sends you to a vast multitude or to twenty-five people, He has called you to be significant. He has called each of us to live in His presence and to stop for the one He puts in front of us each day. God wants to use us, but we have to believe and act upon the revelations He gives us in the secret place.

For instance, Rolland and I had a vision to go to a nation. What would have happened, though, if we had not bought the plane tickets? What if we hadn't wanted to lay our lives down? What if we hadn't lived in God's presence? What if we'd been given this great vision for the poor and the sick but did nothing? What if we hadn't gotten in the Land Rover and spent all those days, weeks, and months driving to unreached villages, at times getting stuck in the mud? What if we hadn't wanted to release the work of that vision to so many hundreds of others? What if we'd tried to do it ourselves?

Our hearts might have been filled with nice revelations, but nothing would have happened if we and our Iris family had not believed Him and responded. Without belief that manifested itself in action, none of that vision would have come through our lives and the lives of those in our movement. We must respond to what God shows us in the secret place—not just for our sake, but also for the sake of all those He wants to touch through us.

Dreams to Drill Wells

One day as I was resting in the secret place, the Lord gave me a vision of freshwater wells and a particular church. Then I felt Him call us to drill wells and put them near the churches.

When God tells us to do something while we are in His presence, we need to respond. We need to go and do what He says. Jesus said, "The Son can do nothing by himself; he can do only what he sees his Father doing" (John 5:19). In His presence God breaks our hearts and opens our eyes to see what He is doing all around us. That is why we cannot go anywhere without Him being present in our lives. If we remain in the secret place, it is first of all because we love Him, but it is also because we are like little children and must watch Him as He shows us what to do.

After I heard God speak to me about the wells, we bought two well-drilling rigs. The church I had seen in my vision paid for one of the rigs. When the rigs arrived, we lost the keys to the first rig almost immediately. The second rig and blaster were transported in two huge containers. The blaster is needed to get through especially hard ground. This was prophetic, because for the next two years both drilling rigs just sat there. We lost the only properly trained engineer we had, who was from India, because officials in the country revoked his visa. Our friend took charge of the project, but before long he, his wife, and his two children were called to leave the country. We tried to get help to operate the drills, but in Southeast Africa this proved difficult, to say the least.

So there we were, with a couple of fine well-drilling rigs no one could get to work. It was pitiful. The means to this great vision were sitting around doing absolutely nothing. We had no technician, no help, not even the keys to start up the rigs.

For two years we contended to see the vision of the wells become a reality. I told God I could not do it alone—just as Moses knew he could not do what God had called him to do by himself (Exod. 33:12). I asked God what to do. The rigs were there, but I had no engineering ability to use them. I knew I had had a real vision, but I didn't know how to make the parts come together. We needed favor. We wanted those wells drilled. We wanted water for everyone thirsting in the nation. Together we continued to trust in God's promise of living water springing forth, spiritually and physically.

At last hope came when a friend of ours told us he knew an engineer who was willing to come from Georgia and help. His name was David. When David arrived, we discovered we had lost another set of keys—this one to access a critical container for the second rig. We had one of our young men cut through the container with a blowtorch!

Soon afterward I drove out to see how our new engineer was coming along. As I pulled up in front of the rigs and got out of the car, he said, "Hi, baby. Do you want to see these machines drill?"

"Sure," I said.

"It is a big miracle," he said. "I can't tell you how big the miracle is. Do you want to see these machines drill, baby?"

At this point I began to wonder where this man had gone to school. I was starting to get worried. I had told everybody that an expert well-drilling engineer had arrived and that we were about to have the drills up and moving. Looking at the man, I suddenly wondered if he was even remotely qualified for the job.

God, of course, can qualify whomever He likes whenever He likes. He can use any yielded lover and any yielded vessel. That is why He was pleased to use Moses—Moses told God he was not going anywhere without His presence (Exod. 33:15). I believe the favor of God upon Moses increased the very moment he said yes and that he would not do it without God's presence. God was looking for a man who would not depend on his own ability, and Moses knew his task was impossible without God's help. He yielded to God's leading because he knew there was no other way to achieve it.

In the same way our most stubborn prayer ought to be, "God, I will do anything You tell me to do—but You have to go with me. I will not live in complacency because of my lack of ability. I will yield myself to You. I trust that You will make me able."

The following Friday David asked me if I felt like I might

preach better on Sunday if the drill rigs were parked outside our local church. I liked that idea and said that I probably would preach better.

That Sunday two huge trucks hauled the rigs in front of the church building. David turned the key, and the drills started running. I saw the ground break right before my eyes. We were giddy with joy. After two long years we finally saw the fulfillment of the dream!

After church we invited David to what I call "holy chaos night." Each Sunday I invite many children to spend the night at our house. We eat chicken, break out Coke bottles, and watch the children play late into the evening. It is very loud, very happy, and always a particularly wild time for any other visitors we might have.

After settling down in the noise and festivity, David turned to my husband and me and said, "Now I am going to tell you the real story, OK? I ain't never finished high school. I have never seen wells—never seen water come out of no hole. But I had a dream. I believed God would use me to drill water wells in Africa. I believed God that I would put those rigs together. I believed God said I was the man for the job! I have a company, and we drill, but we only drill sideways. I never drilled nothing straight down. But I had a dream!"

In just a few days God used David to accomplish a mission that had been disrupted for years. Two other qualified engineers had told me it couldn't be done. Even the government had tried to prevent the drilling. Nonetheless, God sent us a man who believed what was spoken to him in the secret place. He trusted God would give him the ability to put those drill rigs together. He heard God and acted. Thousands of people are now drinking fresh, clean water because one yielded vessel said yes.

Today we have a dedicated well-digging team, including an amazing, qualified Mozambican engineer, and we are continuing to dig new wells in Mozambique.

Remain in the Secret Place

It is important to remain thirsty and to remember God wants to use you. He intends to equip you with His Word and in His presence. This is not a one-time event. It is not like walking into a scheduled meeting from which you can carry away all you will ever require. Becoming familiar with God's Word and His presence is a lifelong journey. The more you experience them, the more desperately you will need them.

The Lord was pleased with Moses because he would not consent to lead Israel without God's presence. We were similarly touched by our friend David's faith—the man who waited in the presence for the Holy Spirit to show him how to put together the drill rigs.

We gave him an honorary doctorate in engineering. It was a tremendous joy for us when we were able to present it to him. Tears streamed down his face. We honored him as a man of God who believed and acted on the strategy he had received from heaven when other men, with all the right degrees, refused to even touch the equipment.

God is pleased to use anyone who believes in Him. He longs to release the keys and strategies from heaven to us in the secret place. His method for changing your nation is *you*. You are the salt. You are the light. You are the person He wants to use.

When we abide in God's presence, the striving and fear in our souls go away. Moses told God, "If you are pleased with me, teach me your ways so I may know you and continue to find favor with you. Remember that this nation is your people" (Exod. 33:13). The Lord replied to him, "My Presence will go with you, and I will give you rest." (v. 14). Then the Lord told Moses what He says to all who are yielded, laid-down lovers—that He will do the very thing we asked because He is pleased with us and knows us by name (v. 17).

We are not nameless to God. He knows us, and He desires us to hear Him calling our names. He taught me this one day as I walked through the village next to our base in Pemba. I had been visiting the neighbors for hours, and I was late for a discipleship meeting. As I hurried down a hill, I noticed a very old lady in rags sitting in the dirt against a mud hut. She was blind. Her eyes were pure white. I felt the Lord asking me to stop for her.

In the local dialect I asked her what her name was. She told me she had none. I thought perhaps she was from another tribe and didn't understand my Makua dialect. I asked her again in a different language, but her answer was the same: "I am blind. I have no name."

There was another woman sitting nearby. I asked her if she knew the blind woman's name, and she too replied: "She is blind, and she has no name."

I was stunned. I hugged the old blind woman and immediately decided that I would call her Utaliya. It means "you exist" or "you are." When I spoke it for the first time, her wrinkled face came alive. She gave me a huge, nearly toothless grin. I asked the other woman nearby to try calling her by the new name. Utaliya turned her white, blind eyes toward that unfamiliar sound and giggled. After that I prayed for her eyes. I watched them turn brown in front of me.

Utaliya could see!

I told her about the man Jesus who had just opened her eyes. I told her about Papa Daddy God, who will always call her by name. She met God that day. I was hours late for my meeting, but it seemed to me I was right on time.

Stay Hungry for His Presence

Most of us have had a vision, calling, or dream from God at one time in our lives. It is likely that not all of what God has shown us has come to pass. If we are to accomplish all He wants for us in this life, we must always desire more of Him. There is always room for more intimacy, more of His presence, and more of His glory.

Our passion will continue to live and burn as long as we cultivate a holy hunger, positioning ourselves to be over-shadowed again and again, looking deep into the eyes of Jesus and eating of Him each day.

I pray that you would be drawn to feast upon God's goodness in the secret place and that you would rest in Him at such a deep level that yielding to His will becomes easy. May you be one who is not content to go anywhere without His presence. In all challenges and all victories I pray that you would seek and find Him. I pray that from within His heart, you would see and stop for each one He places before you. I pray you would live a life of abundant fruitfulness, flowing from intimacy in the secret place.

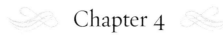

Chapter 4

DEEPER STILL

The man brought me back to the entrance of the temple, and I saw water coming out from under the threshold of the temple toward the east (for the temple faced east). The water was coming down from under the south side of the temple, south of the altar. He then brought me out through the north gate and led me around the outside to the outer gate facing east, and water was flowing from the south side.
—EZEKIEL 47:1–2

There is a river whose streams make glad the city of God, the holy place where the Most High dwells.
—PSALM 46:4

Then the angel showed me the river of the water of life, as clear as crystal, flowing from the throne of God and of the Lamb down the middle of the great street of the city.
—REVELATION 22:1–2

WHAT DOES IT mean to be overshadowed in the secret place? What does it mean to be overtaken and fully possessed by the Holy Spirit? What does it mean to dive deeper into the river flowing from God's heart?

It means our life is not our own. It means we no longer exist for our own desires but for His. Nothing is impossible in a life that is utterly yielded to Him. To be overshadowed means being immersed in the river of life that flows within His Spirit.

God is calling us to go low. He is entreating us to let Him have complete control. He is inviting us to dive deeper into the river of His presence so we can experience true life.

Going Deeper and Lower Still

Ezekiel knew what it meant to go deeper. The waters into which he was invited poured straight from the temple of God, and we also are called to enter them.

The source of the river is God Himself. The river flows from His throne and makes the heavenly city glad. Just as natural rivers always flow into low places, so the river of God always flows into the lowly places. In order to enter it, we have to go lower and lower still. When we are bent down, kneeling down, bowed down, and laid down—then we will find Him. If we are low enough in the Spirit, we will recognize even a trickle of God's presence in a room. We will not be concerned with our position, our place, or anything else that might hinder us. Our overwhelming desire will be full immersion in the river.

I am learning to live in that place of "lower still." I know I am able to go there from inside my room, from a walk in the woods, or from an airplane. I can get there from almost anywhere. The lower I go, the deeper toward the heart of God I find myself. Once I am so low that the waters of His Spirit completely cover me, God takes me beyond all words and all my understanding.

The question for all of us is this: How low do we want to go? How laid down—yielded—do we want to be? I believe we have a choice about how deeply we wish to dive in to God. Whether we are Calvinist, Armenian, or Greek or Russian Orthodox in our theology, we must decide how much we really desire to have union with Him.

God is asking which of us wants to go deeper. Constantly He calls us to greater and greater depths, inviting us to sink down until the river covers us completely and makes our hearts glad.

The angel of the Lord invited Ezekiel to come deeper and deeper still into the water. He measured out a line:

> As the man went eastward with a measuring line in his hand, he measured off a thousand cubits and then led me through water that was ankle-deep. He measured off another thousand cubits and led me through water that was knee-deep. He measured off another thousand and led me through water that was up to the waist.
>
> —EZEKIEL 47:3–4

Ezekiel was likely very frightened by this invitation. Who knows if he could swim or not? When we are ankle-deep in water, we control everything. We can swish and walk around and continue to maintain our balance. We can click our heels, if we like. We can do ministry our own way. We prefer this because we like to be in charge. It disturbs some people, for example, when a speaker loses control and starts sobbing when he or she is supposed to be sharing. I understand this. I know how frightening it can be to feel as if you might be drowning.

But I have been sharing the gospel ceaselessly and

passionately for more than thirty-seven years, and in that time I have learned that you cannot do very much while you are only ankle-deep in the river of God. When you are only ankle-deep, you may still know the Holy Spirit. You may have profound convictions. You may have charismatic gifts. You may see some of God's power. Even so, most of the time you will be confined to activities you know how to produce and control. You will be walking on your own and relying on your own plans.

I know what it is like to have kicked around in ankle- or even knee-deep water for years at a time, not understanding there were deeper places to go. And again I have learned we can do ministry our way in ankle-deep water if we want. But I have also learned we can choose to go as deep as we want to go. God's power and presence are much more powerful than our ability to stand in our own strength. He has deeper places waiting for us than we will ever fully grasp.

Now I always press in to go in deeper. Continually I ask God to take me deep and drown me in His river. God offers an invitation to all who are thirsty to be fully immersed in the glory of His love.

Born for the Water

I was created to live under the waters of the Holy Spirit. In fact, I feel as if I was born to be in the water. I matured in a way opposite that of a frog. At the beginning frogs start out as tadpoles, swimming under the water, and grow up to live on land. I went the other direction. I was like a frog, living on land, and then I became a tadpole. I changed from breathing the air of the world to needing the waters of the Spirit.

I remember the frog life. For years Rolland and I were about waist-deep. We had a total of one very wobbly church to show for it. I imagine frogs can hop in waist-deep water. They have strong legs. I certainly hopped as high as I could for Jesus. I tried so hard to make everything work that my head spun and my heart grew weary.

Then the Lord said, "Come on deeper," and we got one more wobbly church. He said again, "Come on deeper," and we got another wobbly church. Now we had three wobbly churches. We were still hopping with all our might, but we could only get so far being waist-deep in His presence.

Then God showed me an easier way. He showed me I could die to myself. Then He would kiss me back to life, and everything would change.

I believe the Lord is calling us to a lifestyle of laid-down love that goes well beyond being waist-deep in the river. It is a permanent lifestyle of "lower still." It is a call to dive into a love that is limitless, ceaseless, and bottomless—a call to relinquish control.

"Deeper still" is a place of both death and life. The Lord wants to love you to death and kiss you to life. But this cannot happen by your own strength or design. It is exclusively the gift of an intimate relationship with Him.

Do you want to live in the ankle-deep presence of God, or do you want to be immersed in Him? Do you want to go around hopping for God through strain and effort, or do you want to learn how to swim? Do you want to be so fully immersed in His presence that you begin to see what burns in His heart? Would you allow yourself to be confronted with His pain over all this world's multitudes of lost, lonely, hungry, and dying people?

It is when you become immersed in the love of the Father that you truly begin to love like Jesus. He wants to immerse you. He wants to hold you. He wants to take you to a place where you are so far over your head in the river of God that miracles happen all around you. He wants to fill you entirely with His Holy Spirit.

How Deep Will You Go?

> He measured off another thousand, but now it was a river that I could not cross, because the water had risen and was deep enough to swim in—a river that no one could cross.
>
> —EZEKIEL 47:5

I wonder—how deep in this river did Ezekiel want to go? Ankle-deep, waist-deep, neck-deep? Did he long to go all the way in? In the end the angel of the Lord took Ezekiel into a river too deep to cross. The current was too powerful and the waters too high for him to have any stability besides the Lord.

Diving all the way into the river means we have no more ability to stand on our own. There is nowhere to set our feet. It takes complete surrender. And God wants to take us beyond what we can control. He wants to take us to a place where we can be moved in any direction purely by the flow of His presence.

Anyone who has ever worked in our ministry understands we are in way over our heads. It bothers some people. In fact, we are so in over our heads that if God does not show up through supernatural provision, people will go hungry. Every day thousands of children look to us for their daily meals. We cannot continue do this without divine intervention. We literally have to trust God our Father for our daily bread. We have no backup plan. We simply keep leaning deeper and deeper into the goodness of the Lord.

Whenever I am home in Pemba, I like to swim out in the ocean. It is one of my favorite ways to get into the secret place. Beneath the water it is easy to feel hidden in God. There are no distractions.

I try to get as far from shore as I can. If anyone spots me and tries to chase me, I swim faster. If they yell my name, I go where I cannot hear them anymore. If I am going to be good for anything during the rest of the week, I absolutely require this time. I stay desperate for that time with God.

Under the waves I ask God to teach me how I can live in the river without interruption. I want to be fully immersed in the Holy Spirit. I want to be completely covered until no one will see me, but only Christ in me. Even in that place, when I am totally hidden and the Holy Spirit fills each breath, I long to go deeper still.

I also love to scuba dive, and I like to go as far down toward the reefs as I can. When I dive, I have to strap on weights so I can stay underwater without effort; if I don't wear weights, I'll have to constantly kick my legs, swimming downward to keep from floating back to the surface.

The glory of the Lord can sometimes feel like a heavy weight, and that very weight is a gift. It helps us sink low into the deep places and stay there without strain. Without the heavy glory of the Lord upon us, we cannot find the lowest place.

When I dive, I get to experience a new and different realm. Through my mask a different world greets me, like another dimension. God's kingdom too is a different realm, and when He calls us there, He is calling us to a new dimension. If we want to stay there, we have to be able to breathe underwater.

One day the Lord spoke right as I stepped off the dry land and into the ocean. I felt Him say, "It's that easy to live in the realm of the kingdom. Is this deep enough for you?"

I said, "No, Lord."

Then I felt Him say, "Come deeper still."

I stepped farther into the water over shallow rocks and sand. I waded in until I was up to my waist and felt Him say, "Now allow Me to carry you." I let myself go all the way into the water. Just like that another reality covered and surrounded me.

Allowing God to carry us when we don't understand what's happening can feel frightening. Sometimes we may feel as if we're about to drown. He comforts us only by promising that when we let go, we actually will die. After death, however, there is new resurrection life. Even after coming to know Jesus as our Savior, there remains a place of "deeper still." We can go on to become totally immersed in the realm of our Father's love.

Some may hesitate, make excuses, and step away because the prospect of immersion looks dangerous. Some will think they are not ready to swim that far down and will wonder why they're being thrown into deep water when they don't even know how to swim. I believe that the Lord would tell you not to worry. If you jump in, He will catch you, and then you will drown in His deep love. Whenever we do choose to jump, He will pull us right down so we are forced to learn how to breathe in the Holy Spirit's realm.

God is calling us to be a people who can breathe under-water. We have kept our heads above water long enough. Being in over our heads and out of control is precisely what He wants.

Beneath the surface, the plants and wildlife are very different. At first everything about the environment seems incredibly strange. I feel that the Lord is inviting us into a place we have been afraid to live in—the supernatural realm of His kingdom, where His manifest presence surrounds and holds us like water in the ocean's depths.

We were created to breathe in this realm. We can be permanently immersed in the glory of His love. We simply have to drown.

When I try to surface and breathe outside the place of His heart, it no longer feels right to me. If I come up and feel the atmosphere of human religion, it hurts me. I sink back down inside His heart, and I ask Him to keep me there. I've also learned that if you live immersed in the Spirit, you do not get so exhausted. The hardest time to walk is when coming out of the water. You have to be careful when walking over the coral and rock. When you are knee-deep and waist-deep, it's hard to move. You are half in the water and half in the world. Once you are floating, you enter into a whole new kind of freedom.

God wants to accustom you to a different realm because your real home is not here. Being in the African bush is an unspeakable joy for me, but it is not my home. My home is in another place. My heart is with the One I love. I spend so much of my life trying to swim down deeper that the reality of this earth is not mine anymore. My reality is completely solid, concrete, and real to me, but it is not this one. This is why at times I see things differently from the way others see them.

God is looking for a people He can so immerse in His love that for the rest of their lives they will have to survive inside His heart. Nothing else will matter to them. In this secret place you can hear the heartbeat of God for yourself. He will tell you the things that delight His heart. He will call you to go and to do whatever He wants, and you will not refuse Him.

He knows it is frightening. Still, He calls us deeper. No matter how deep we have gone, there is more. We need to go deeper and lower until all we have is the mind of Christ. We are called to be more than a people who can dive for brief periods but have to keep popping up our heads, trying to figure it all out. We have to be able to breathe in His atmosphere without coming up for the world's air.

Let God take you into that place. Do not allow it to remain a matter of mere words. Ask Him to transform you in His love. Worship Him and wait upon Him until you are overwhelmed to the point of no return. If you drink daily from the river of God and stay immersed in Him, then with increasing measure you will begin to pour out a love that is irresistible. As you minister to the broken, the dying, and the hurting, God's holy presence will overflow and spill forth with peace and joy through every part of your life.

I pray that God will continue to immerse you in His love until the only thing you understand anymore is His heart. I challenge you to make a lifelong commitment to go deeper still each and every day.

I encourage you to pray with me now and say, "God, I'm

not satisfied. I cannot live ankle-, knee-, or waist-deep. I must be completely immersed in Your presence. Lord, here I am. Immerse me. I do not want to keep from drowning. I want to drown in Your love. I want to know what it is to be immersed and undone. I want to know what it is to be out of control and for You to be totally and completely in control. Lord, come like a rushing river. I invite You to sweep me away to deeper places."

Life in the Dark Places

He asked me, "Son of man, do you see this?" Then he led me back to the bank of the river. When I arrived there, I saw a great number of trees on each side of the river. He said to me, "This water flows toward the eastern region and goes down into the Arabah, where it enters the Sea. When it empties into the Sea, the water there becomes fresh. Swarms of living creatures will live wherever the river flows. There will be large numbers of fish, because this water flows there and makes the salt water fresh; so where the river flows everything will live."

—EZEKIEL 47:6–9

A great outpouring in my nation of Mozambique began in the midst of a flood that brought vast destruction. It was so bad in the villages that there were instances of women having to give birth to their babies in trees. We went out with helicopters, Land Rovers, and boats to help as many as we could. When we had to, we went wading through the water on foot.

As we did this, hundreds of thousands of people started

coming to Jesus. People were desperate. This terrible flood brought one of the greatest spiritual changes the land has ever seen.

God tells us that if we would let Him give us His heart and mind, then we could also begin to do what He does. Jesus only did what the Father was doing. He said, "I tell you the truth, the Son can do nothing by himself; he can do only what he sees his Father doing, because whatever the Father does the Son also does. For the Father loves the Son and shows him all he does. Yes, to your amazement he will show him even greater things than these" (John 5:19).

His river flows through us as a consequence of the intimate love found in the secret place. We have to enter this river for ourselves in order to get to the life that is found there. Once we are immersed in His river, life will also follow us wherever we go—even into the darkest of places.

When we live in the river of God, totally immersed in His heart, healing is released through us. Rich life springs up along the banks and the shores of our lives. Pure water from God transforms and purifies any other murky waters we may face. It makes salty or bitter waters fresh.

When we went from three churches to thousands of churches in a few short years, it was because God immersed us in His Spirit in a way we had never known before. Many people ask how it happened. I can only tell them that God did it. There is not much else to say. He looked at us—little people laid down in the dirt so low that even the smallest stream of His presence would have been able to flow over our heads—and He blessed us all. He poured out His Holy Spirit and sent a host of beautiful ministers to our movement. As it says in the Ezekiel passage above, swarms of creatures and fish were found in this river.

God has given us a powerful promise: Wherever the river flows, life will thrive. Imagine abundant life, healing, and joy released without measure in every place we set our feet. I believe that is exactly what is to come as we learn, together, to abide in the river.

Before the Mozambique floods we used to lead people to the Lord a few at a time. Now they come in swarms. Often almost whole villages receive Jesus overnight. I remember one village where there was not a single Christian. As I prepared to speak there for the first time, I remembered the Ezekiel passage above. I believed with all my heart that through the love of the Father, we were going to bring living water to the village that day.

Normally night brings pitch darkness to the villages, but we had brought a generator. The spiritual atmosphere of that particular village felt unusually grim, but we had brought our own children from our children's center, and they are very hard to depress. We set up lights and a speaker system. The children spoke, sang, and played the drums in a long stretch of exuberant worship. I also spoke. When I was done, I said, "Bring me the blind and the deaf!"

There were no deaf people—that's a rarity in our part of Africa. But soon someone came to me and told me that they did know a blind man who was also paralyzed. He was in his hut because he could not get there.

That was perfect. I borrowed a flashlight and set out with my prayer team of children to the man's hut. When we arrived, we met the blind man. He was wrapped up in a sheet covered in bright blue cartoon Smurfs! I have always wondered how he got that Smurf sheet or if anyone in the village even knew what Smurfs were. I suppose it did not matter much to him at the time.

We sat around him, prayed for him, and hugged him. He stayed blind. Then he said he had a headache. We prayed for his headache, and that went away, but he still could not see.

I asked him if he wanted to know Jesus. He and his whole family were ready to surrender their lives to Jesus, he told me. I remember thinking, "He does not even see, but he still wants Jesus. That is wonderful faith." The man and his whole family met Jesus that night.

Before I left his hut, I told him, "When you see tomorrow, please send me a runner back to Pemba with the news."

Pemba, where I live, is many hours away from this village. That night I was surely not thinking like a normal person would. I was immersed in God's presence, so I thought and spoke differently than a person in the natural world would. That was a good thing too, because the rest of the evening was incredibly challenging. A few of the villagers began to stone us and our children. The visitors we had brought along with us locked themselves in my Land Rover. They said they were interceding for us.

One of our young girls ignored the rocks and asked for the blind to come and be healed. Some of the friendlier villagers brought one more blind man to us. She and I prayed, and that man received his sight instantly. The man had held to another faith moments before being healed, but at once he yelled, "Hallelujah," grabbed the nearest microphone, and began speaking about Jesus to the crowd. He said, "The One they are talking about is real. I was blind and now I can see!"

After that many people in the village received Jesus.

All this happened on a Thursday night. By Sunday no runners had come to Pemba with news that the first blind man could see. I was a little bit confused about this. I fully expected him to be healed.

On Monday I was talking with a friend, a man who happens to be an influential businessman in Pemba. This friend practices another religion. We were parked in his car on our Glory Base when a stranger suddenly came up to the truck and tapped on the window. My friend was a bit suspicious and wanted me to ask the stranger what he was doing. It is not always safe to talk to strangers in Pemba.

I did not know what this was about, but I rolled down my window to ask. As soon as I lowered the window, the stranger said, "I am the runner!" Then another one came up beside him, blurting, "He can see! And he can walk too. He is on his land, farming!"

My businessman friend asked me to pray for him then and there. He took my hand and laid it on his own eyes. Whatever I had, he wanted.

Sometimes God will allow you to wait and wonder why He is not doing something exactly when you thought He would. Sometimes God is only asking you to wait until Monday. He knows what He is doing. Because the runners arrived at that precise time, my friend from another faith was convinced that he needed to experience Jesus.

God is very much in control even if His way of doing things is unexpected. That is why we stay under the river's waters.

Spread Wide Your Nets

Fishermen will stand along the shore; from En Gedi to En Eglaim there will be places for spreading nets. The fish will be of many kinds—like the fish of the

Great Sea....Fruit trees of all kinds will grow on both banks of the river. Their leaves will not wither, nor will their fruit fail. Every month they will bear fruit, because the water from the sanctuary flows to them. Their fruit will serve for food and their leaves for healing.

—EZEKIEL 47:10, 12

On each side of the river stood the tree of life, bearing twelve crops of fruit, yielding its fruit every month. And the leaves of the tree are for the healing of the nations.

—REVELATION 22:2

There are "fish" all around us, waiting to be captured in the net of the Father's love. Horrible things have happened in this generation, but that is all the more reason to spread our nets in faith and believe that we are going to bring in multitudes.

People are always spreading fishing nets in front of our children's base in Pemba, which is located right on the ocean. Usually ten to twenty women will spread a single massive net. These nets are far too big for any one person to handle. They get covered in weights to anchor them to the ocean floor, and at the end of the day I watch the people come back and sing together as they haul in the catch. Because they work together, the process looks effortless.

Our time for taking up a fishing pole and waiting three hours to catch one fish is over. It is not a time for one or two super-anointed evangelists to dominate the work of the harvest. It is a time for us to cooperate in laying down the vast nets God has placed in our hands. We do not need to strive to the breaking point. We simply need to be hidden inside His heart and work together. God loves it when different streams of the church join in love to take in His net. I believe He is raising up an army of laid-down lovers who will each hold on to his or her part of the net in order to bring in fish by the millions.

The trees rooted on the banks of the river flowing from the sanctuary of God bear fruit every month of the year. This is a supernatural process. If we stay immersed, God will cause us to yield fruit at a supernatural pace.

Fruitfulness is birthed from love. Bearing fruit is a delight, but it is not the final goal. Intimacy with God must be our purpose. If we pursue Him above all else, fruit simply happens. I have never seen a fruit tree push hard and say, "Give me fruit!" Trees have no other task than to stand rooted in the soil. They soak up the waters that flow from the heart of God, and new life grows.

People often ask us how they too can grow thousands of churches within a few years, as has happened in Mozambique. We laugh. We do not know how to do it. At Iris we simply love God, love our neighbors, and spend time in God's presence. He is the one who chose to use us.

One man can probably control a church of fifty if he works hard and subjects himself to a lot of stress. He can bear fruit in season. However, the person who gives control to God opens himself to the possibility of untimely fruitfulness. Those who choose this way lay their whole lives upon the altar, willing to be taken anywhere and be given any task.

When you dive into the deep waters, there are twelve months of fruitfulness waiting for you. There is life and healing. You are going to know what to do and how to do it, as you remain immersed in the heart of God. Learn to stay hidden in Him, and you will be surrounded by the supernatural fruit of His love.

Chapter 5

REMAIN *in* HIM

> *I am the true vine, and my Father is the gardener. He cuts off every branch in me that bears no fruit, while every branch that does bear fruit he prunes so that it will be even more fruitful. You are already clean because of the word I have spoken to you. Remain in me, and I will remain in you. No branch can bear fruit by itself; it must remain in the vine. Neither can you bear fruit unless you remain in me. I am the vine; you are the branches. If a man remains in me and I in him, he will bear much fruit; apart from me you can do nothing.*
>
> —JOHN 15:1–5

A T ALL TIMES God desires to increase our fruitfulness. If we want to live yielded to Him, He will also prune us so this can happen. This can seem painful to us at times because we do not understand exactly what is going on. But while He is pruning us above the ground, He is also multiplying our root system below. As He cuts off unyielding branches, our roots dig ever deeper.

In the first twenty years of our ministry we felt we had

produced little fruit. We planted three churches and saw a few miracles, but we felt that the visible fruit of our later years would not be much greater than this. At times this was discouraging to us because it did not match our hopes. I used to think I would probably prefer to become a martyr for Christ before too long. Life was hard. I wanted to go home soon. I was ready to kneel before God and give Him what fruit I had. Even if I could only bring Him one little grape, I knew that grape was precious to Him because I had worked my whole life for it.

But God wanted more than a grape from me. He wanted a vineyard. He showed me how much more fruitful it would be to live for Him than to die before my time. And I found out that one of the ways to cultivate the vineyard is to invite Him to prune me.

Allow Yourself to Be Pruned

Jesus is the true vine, and His Father is the gardener. Because of the Father's desire to see us flourish, He has to cut off every branch that bears no fruit. This hurts, but it comes from love. We would do well to take a posture before God that allows Him to prune anything and everything in us. Since we are called and chosen to be radical lovers who will carry the gospel to the ends of the earth, our destiny is to bear His glory. His desire is to remove anything that hinders this goal.

Sometimes He chops off things we love. Sometimes He removes things we thought we liked. While He cuts off these branches and we start to feel the pain, He keeps on going while covering us with His kindness. This kind of discipline always releases us into greater measures of our destiny.

God has delivered me from some things that used to bind me. He has cut away that which I used to think was there for a good reason. He looks gently at me, even though I may yell out in pain. He sees the end result and knows it is better than I can imagine.

If we do not understand His heart, passages such as John 15:1–2 might cause us to imagine God is mean. The God who holds a machete or pruning knife may not sound very cuddly—but the truth is that He is eternally gracious. He may chop and burn pieces of us, but when He does this, He will hold you in His arms and let you know He loves you.

After more than thirty-seven years of missions, I am starting to understand that every time He has chopped and burned anything in my life and those in our ministry, it has brought more fruitfulness. Even if we have to change things that are very painful to change, we always say yes.

The Lord has been pruning my life for many years. After I was powerfully touched in Toronto, I felt Him say to me, "I want more time with you. I am going to have to cut away the things in your schedule that are not important to Me." While I lay stuck to the floor, I could no longer play at church. I could not stay busy with any of the traditional activities. I could not talk or move, much less sing or preach or testify.

While I lay there, I wondered how fruitful that could possibly be. But after that experience of intimate love, fruit started growing exponentially. God blessed us by showing us every miracle we had ever dreamed about.

The relentless drivenness in my personality did not leave me after my encounter at Toronto, but I found out it was one of many things that had to change. This was a hard process. I felt so ready to take on the world! I thought, "Let's take on India, Congo, and Sudan—yes!" I was saying yes all the time, no matter what. Yes! Go! Yes! Go!

But God had to chop. He told me He was going to cut away, He was going to burn, and He was going to prune the things in my life that needed to go.

I responded to God that there was one thing I would not negotiate.

Now, it is not the smartest thing to tell God what you will and will not do. I do not suggest it to anyone. Even so, I told Him the one thing I always had to do was live with all of the children. At that time we had hundreds of children living with us at our children's center. It was an incredibly loud place, and I had very little time to myself there, but I loved being close to all that was going on. I thrive on holy chaos.

At once I felt the Lord wooing and cutting away. He wanted to take me away and put me in a peaceful place instead. There was a home available to buy five minutes from our center, but I resisted. I had always lived in community among the people and all of my children. I thought maybe the anointing would lift if I lived away from them.

But the Lord insisted. I felt Him leading my husband and me to move away from our base into a house that was five minutes down the street. I asked if I could at least bring eight of our boys there, but I felt Him tell us they could stay with us on weekends. Our own two children were already grown up and studying at university.

God was calling me to come away with Him and spend more time in worship—more time in the secret place.

As I invite His pruning, I can step out of myself. It is

what allows me to look into the eyes of a hungry child or a dying grandmother and realize there is truly always enough. I agreed with the Lord that I would give Him the most precious time in my day, no matter how much the world and the church and the people pressed in to take it away.

I have learned that we are called to resist the unnecessary demands of the world. Sometimes we need to cry out to God to keep us from giving in to earthly pressures. I invite the fire. I invite the pruning knife. I encourage you to be one who *loves* first and *does* later.

There is nothing I would not do for Him. There is no place I would not go for Him. There is nothing I would not give to Him. If that is the case for you, He wants your time at least as much as He wants mine!

When He asks me to take a long walk and worship Him, I gladly go. When He draws me into the ocean to look at the fish, I get my snorkel and dive in. I will go and worship underwater for hours if He calls me there. Some people might think I'm lazy by doing this, but I know more good fruit comes from this love affair than I could ever produce otherwise.

The Lord is asking you to give Him your time for the sake of love. What would it look like if we laid our precious cell phones and laptops on the altar before Him even for an hour or so each day? What if we truly prioritized Him above everything else?

One by one He is asking the whole church, "Who has the time to let Me woo him into the secret place? Who will lie down until he is so immersed in My love and My glory that when he stands up again, fruit will spring up all around?"

I encourage you to say, "Here am I, Lord. Cut away everything you want to cut. Burn off everything you want to burn. Lord, rearrange my schedule."

It might not be your mornings that you give Him but your evenings. It might be your lunchtime or your Saturday. I believe some are literally called to live in mountain cabins for seasons and spend entire days in worship. Others are called to foreign nations. Some are called to the inner cities; others to go into hospitals as physicians or to universities as professors, deans, and presidents. Each one of us has a unique call and destiny that the Lord shows us as we spend time with Him.

But all of us are called to spend time in the secret place. Not one person stands outside that call.

I remember struggling once when God called me by saying, "Come away, My beloved, and walk on the beach."

My little religious heart struggled with that invitation. Going to a pretty beach was difficult for me to handle—I felt guilty because I was not sacrificing very much in a task like that. I thought maybe it would be holier if I shut my eyes to the grandeur of land and sea. Yet I knew He had called me, so I finally decided I was going to open my eyes and simply thank Him for the beauty around me.

I understand now that God wants to cut away things that are falsely religious in our lives. He is not concerned about how strictly we can deprive ourselves. He is concerned that our hearts be filled with passion for Him.

It is good to let Jesus cut away the branches in us that do not bear fruit, but sometimes even the branches that *do* bear fruit need pruning so we can become even more fruitful. He asks only that we trust Him. Abundant fruit is the result of surrender, and any life that is laid down for the sake of love is a ministry life.

Let Him chop away anything and everything for love's sake, but do not be harsh with yourself for any lesser reason. Sell your cars, houses, and everything else to move across the world—but only if you do it for love. It will be enough. One person living a life of radical obedience for love's sake can bear enough fruit to capture many hearts for Jesus.

Fresh Bread and Sweet Fruit

Would you want to live on stale crumbs or rotten fruit? Most people don't like crumbs or stale bread, yet sometimes that's what we offer people when we don't minister out of a real fruitfulness in our lives. Starving people run to church, get some stale crumbs from us in an hour-long time slot, and then wonder why they're not full. Just as there is a fragrance to fresh bread that causes hungry children (or even the rich!) to come, there is something about fruit fresh from the vine that attracts people in need. People welcome us when it becomes clear we have the sort of food they're craving.

If you will pay the cost and remain in Him, you will always have spiritual food to give to your family and city. You will have fresh bread and fruit. There will be more than enough. This is our destiny, as long as we understand we cannot bear the least of this fruit without seeking Him daily.

We can do absolutely nothing without Him. Nothing! Not a single grape can be found to give to the Father without Jesus. He is the vine, and we are the branches.

When we hold to Him, our fruit will be sweet and whole-some and have no worms. People will not be afraid of us. They will be eager for the nourishment we bring from the Lord.

We must be living trees, letting our shade help people live in love and intimacy. We need to encourage one another toward increasing freedom. We need not make the task too complicated. We are called to abide in His presence and to love others. We stop before Him in the secret place, and then we stop to love the person who is in front of us as we go about our day.

We must remain in Him at all costs. This means yielding to Him when He speaks and obeying Him. It also means learning to rest in Him.

Once, when I was particularly exhausted from a busy week, I decided it was time to make a promise to my young assistant Shara. I made a covenant with her that I would model rest for her generation. I told her I would change my schedule and cut back. I told her I would do less so I could spend more time in God's presence.

Sometimes it is a difficult promise to keep, but it burned in my heart as I made it.

Around that same time two of my watches malfunc-tioned in two days. The first watch, a very reliable model, stopped for no apparent reason. I bought another cheaper one at the airport. The same thing happened to that one the next day. I believe God was showing me that if I would do less, He would do more.

No is not always a popular word, but saying yes to God sometimes requires saying no to people who want things from us. We must be able to yield, not caring what it costs us to obey radically and love without limits. We must lay our lives on the altar and, for love's sake, obey.

God has given many of us visions and prophecies. Some of us have received amazing visitations, read encouraging scriptures, and had the most incredible ideas. As we position ourselves on the altar in a place of abandoned love, let's ask the Lord to give us hearts that are totally fixed on His face—hearts that choose to remain in Him always.

Many people have had heavenly visitations or have received impressive-sounding prophetic words about being called to many nations, great ministries, or the media. But before all these things God asks us to make a covenant of obedience. Much of the time we do not need any new revelations, however powerful they may be. We need to abide in Him and obey the commands we have already been given.

There are as many incredible callings as there are people, and you may well already have yours. Often we do not need another vision for ourselves so much as we need to lay everything we have on the altar. If we would do what we already know we are called to do, the world would be shaken to its core. This can and will happen as we remain in Him. To abide in His love is to obey Him.

God has called you to abide and remain in Him, the true vine, the source of all life. Who cares what it costs? *Of course* it will cost everything. You can expect that, but how much would you give for eternal love? Where would you go? What would you do?

Learning to Abide

I admit that as a movement we are not always abiding as deeply as we could be, but together we are learning how to abide in the One who is altogether beautiful. This is why we cannot write a neat ten-step process for bearing fruit. We cannot create God's kind of fruitfulness. Perfect fruit comes from the perfect One. Our desire must be to enter His heart and love Him until fruit appears.

It is backward to try to love Him for the sake of fruit. Rather, we should desire fruit because we love Him. We are still learning more about this, but our goal is not to oversee some kind of world-leading church-growth movement. Our one desire is to be in love with Him and to love Him well, and then to love every man, woman, and child we meet each day. All we really want is for our love to burn for Him, because we know that His love burns for us. He is for us. If we will yield, He will not let anything dead remain in us.

He says, "If anyone does not remain in me, he is like a branch that is thrown away and withers; such branches are picked up, thrown into the fire and burned" (John 15:6). And so not only will He prune us, but He will also take every branch that does not bear fruit and burn it up. Everything that does not bring Him pleasure or that would lead to disobedience is going to be thrown into the fire. Before our eyes He is going to burn away anything that would hinder us. He is so in love with us that He will not allow dead branches to hang from our trees. His passion for us is too fierce and too jealous to let us squander our lives outside of connection to Himself, the true vine.

We each have dreams and destinies. I pray God would

burn away everything that does not bring Him pleasure—any desire that does not make His heart sing. I pray God would take us further into the secret place. When we do not know what to do or how to do it, I pray He would simply help us to yield more completely to Him. As He prunes us, He invites us into deeper intimacy. He invests Himself in our very dreams.

As we remain in Him, we get to know His heart more, and our desires become aligned with His. Jesus says, "If you remain in me and my words remain in you, ask whatever you wish, and it will be given you" (John 15:7). What do you find yourself wanting when you abide in Him? This can be a perplexing question to ask, but I believe God trusts you. In this place He says we can ask of Him whatever we want. Do you want an unreached people group to know Jesus? Do you want a whole university to come to know His love? Do you want a cure for malaria?

You may be thinking you really want a yacht—but is that actually what you want? When you are in the holy place, in worship, in the heart of Jesus, what do you *really* want? When we are abiding in Him, our motives and actions are made clear. Once they are revealed, we find pure and simple desires. We might say we want the whole Makua tribe to be saved or maybe the whole Hollywood industry to be touched by the Lord.

The Lord's response is, "Let's go get them!"

I remember a time when I fell so deeply into the secret place that I felt God tell me to ask Him for anything I wanted. Some people think He should only be telling us what *He* wants. He does this too, but this time He was very definitely asking me what *I* wanted.

I told Him I wanted to see our movement care for a

million children in my lifetime. I wanted to find all the children who were dying of starvation and bring them into a home. He liked that idea! I think maybe He even thought of it.

You see, when you spend time with Him in the secret place, a union takes place that causes you to start thinking like God. You begin to have His thoughts. You take on the mind of Christ. He finds it awesome that I want to care for a million children. I could have asked for a BMW, and I think I probably would have gotten one, but I wanted something else. In the secret place I had a mind connected with the presence and the purposes of God. I wanted children.

I also told Him I wanted to see a youth army—a generation of radical, laid-down lovers in the kingdom of God who would not burn out but would instead burn upward. Rolland and I want to see a people who run the race to the end. We want to see our ceiling become their floor; then we want to bust through our ceiling and run faster than them so they have to speed up to catch us! We want to see this army of lovers released into their giftings. We want to see the old embrace the young and the rich embrace the poor. We want to see wars stop and love conquer hatred.

We have a vision. We have a dream, and it came in the secret place. We fix our eyes on Jesus. In that place of union God said I could ask for anything I wanted. He will give it to us. He wants to take you into that place too. When you are there, you will realize you must remain in Him for life.

Bearing good fruit demonstrates to the world we are truly His disciples (John 15:8). A tree has to brave the wind, rain, and storm to release its fruit. It can be strong enough for this purpose only when it is deeply rooted in the soil. By remaining in Him, we allow Him to cultivate the soil beneath us. Each month as we rest in the river—careful to abide in obedience, spending time in the secret place—He promises to produce more and more good fruit through us.

Our Father takes great pleasure when we release fruit that gives life to everyone around us. Give Him the time He asks for. Enter into His presence each day. Feast upon the fresh bread, which is Jesus. Welcome the process of His pruning, knowing He sees a bigger picture. Yield every cell in your body.

He is your life source. He is the true vine. Without Him we can do nothing of any worth or lasting value, but He is glorified as we bear fruit from Him, with Him, and in Him.

Chapter 6

PAYING *the* PRICE

> *This is how the birth of Jesus Christ came about: His mother Mary was pledged to be married to Joseph, but before they came together, she was found to be with child through the Holy Spirit. Because Joseph her husband was a righteous man and did not want to expose her to public disgrace, he had in mind to divorce her quietly.*
>
> *But after he had considered this, an angel of the Lord appeared to him in a dream and said, "Joseph son of David, do not be afraid to take Mary home as your wife, because what is conceived in her is from the Holy Spirit. She will give birth to a son, and you are to give him the name Jesus, because he will save his people from their sins."*
>
> —MATTHEW 1:18–21

MARY HAD TO bear the reproach of being pregnant with God's promise every day for many months. I think wherever she walked, she had to cope with looks, whispers, accusations, and insults among her friends and community—probably even among her own family. She had to continue to carry the promise when everyone thought it obvious she was unclean. She persevered when no one understood her or the incredible gift she carried. She had to endure shame, slander, and ridicule. In the midst of this suffering she continued to say yes to God. She nurtured the miracle of God within her.

Expectant mothers often feel stretched and pulled. Going through the discomfort of carrying the baby's extra weight is part of the process. Even when circumstances are good, it is not easy. There are nights when mothers cannot sleep and days when they cannot eat. There is the pain of birth. But all turns to joy when the baby arrives!

A Call to Sacrifice

Another occasion in my life when the Lord especially overshadowed me was at a church conference in Red Deer, Canada. At that time we had spent twelve years in Asia, three in England, and eight in Mozambique. I was about to speak, and as usual I was getting ready by lying prostrated on the ground with my arms stretched out to God. I was crying out to Him, telling Him that even if He called me to go to Laguna Beach, California—to the rich—I would go.

I said this because, for me, that would be a hard sacrifice! I much prefer being with the poor, but I was ready to sacrifice. I was crying out, "Take me and use me! Bruise me, if need be."

Suddenly I felt as if I was being pulled inside the Lord's heart. I heard His next words clearly: "Go and get my lost Makua bride." I did not know the first thing about who the Makua were, but immediately my heart was broken for them.

As had happened with similar encounters in the past, I could not talk or walk afterward. That night I had to be carried to the car. Later, when I was able to speak again, I called my husband, Rolland, and asked him to research who the Makua were. A few hours later he called me back and told me they were the most unreached tribal group in southeast Africa. Millions of Makua people happened to live in the far north of Mozambique.

I realized that to reach them, we would have to leave the southern part of the country. I began to feel the weight and pain of what God had asked us to do. We would have to leave behind most of the children at our southern base. We had found many of those children in the garbage dumps and street corners of Maputo. We loved them dearly. I cried out to God about it, and He told me we could take fifty of them with us to the north.

It took us a while to get ready and train our southern team, who would continue the base there, but about one year later a few staff, fifty children, and Rolland and I moved to the town of Pemba in the northern province of Cabo Delgado. At that time we had no northern base, no buildings, and nowhere permanent to live. I found myself once again sharing the gospel on street corners.

Who will carry His promise? Who burns with His heart for the lost? Who will say yes, even when stretched and pulled, inconvenienced and made uncomfortable? Who will say yes to carrying His love—whether to those who are obviously poor, naked, wretched, and blind, or to those who think they are rich but are really penniless? Who will go and get His lost bride in North Korea or at Yale University?

When God comes and overshadows us, we are

experiencing God touching human flesh. Can you put a price on that? How much could we possibly pay?

Will you carry the beauty of Jesus to a dying world?

Most of the greatest miracles Rolland and I have ever witnessed occurred during our most difficult personal trials. When our circumstances were the most stressful, food started multiplying. The blind started to see. The deaf started to hear. Some of our pastors saw people raised · from the dead.

People have shot at us, thrown us in jail, and kicked us out of our homes. I have been shipwrecked, beaten, car-jacked, stoned, and threatened with knives and guns. In fact, I can no longer count the number of times my life has been threatened. When it happens now, I often laugh. Being in love with God brings a fearlessness that surpasses understanding. He is worth it all!

"Let Mama Go!"

Once in Mozambique I was walking down the street with my prayer team. On that day the team happened to be made up of young girls, eight to ten years old. Without warning a truckload of police raced up the street and pulled up in front of us. Eight men with assault rifles pointed them at my head. They told me to get in the truck. They were going to take me to jail because I had recently been preaching in the prisons without permission.

I laughed at them. "Are we really that scary? Does it take eight of you with AK-47s to come get me and my little girls?" I asked.

They did not appreciate being laughed at. A few cocked their guns in my face.

I refused to get in the truck. I told them I would walk with them alongside their truck to go to jail. Meanwhile my girls were crying, "Don't shoot Mama Aida!"

I walked to the station with them behind the truck. When we got there, they put me in a room. Then my girls went and rounded up some of my friends—the bandits, prostitutes, and gang leaders. These people do not much like the local jail. They should know—they spend a lot of time there. My little girls got together with these more colorful friends of mine and gathered in a small mob outside the jail. They started shouting, "Let Mama go! Let Mama go! Let Mama go!"

The police were astonished. "You're the mama to them all?" they asked me.

I said, "Yes. They're my spiritual children. They're works in progress!"

The police chief who really wanted me in jail had been called away for an emergency, so the police let me go but told me I had to come back the next day at eight in the morning.

I arrived early, which almost never happens with me. I felt like the Holy Spirit told me to go in at eight o'clock sharp. I did not know the reason why, but I obeyed. When I walked in, the policeman in charge threw up his hands and said, "I cannot believe this happened *again!*"

The chief had just left on emergency business right when he was needed for a second time. I asked the ranking policeman what his name was. He told me, and it was a biblical name. I asked if I could tell him the story of his name. I shared about this policeman's namesake and prayed for Him to meet Jesus, and at once the Holy Spirit fell on him.

I told him I could not stay in jail because I had to go

minister in Australia. My plane was leaving soon. Not only did the policeman let me go, but he also spoke to his police chief on our behalf. That month Iris Global received an official letter allowing us to minister in all the jails and prisons in that province.

What could they do? What can anyone do when you are fearless? When you cannot be made to fit into preconceived boxes, even people who want to think of you as an enemy will not know what to do with you. But you can be truly fearless only when you are in love—when you are immersed and yielded to the point that you do not care about the cost.

If you are always in the river, always in love, and always ready to pay any price, it doesn't matter what the world does to you. In the secret place you do not fear being shot at or killed. Jesus has become utterly real to you. If you die, you go to heaven.

The world will not understand. They don't know what to do with the kind of fearlessness that comes from being drowned in His love. You will need this courage. When God puts a dream inside your heart, you can expect that it will cost you something. The destiny He wants to release through your life is no light matter. It is the most joyful thing you can ever do, but it is also a sacred mandate to practice sacrificial love.

Rolland and Heidi Baker

A Bit of History

Heidi's college graduation picture,
spring 1979—ready to preach the gospel!

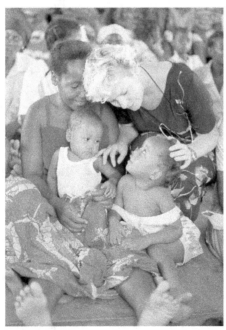

Heidi feeding flood victims at a Maputo cashew factory, 2000

Early baptisms at Chihango Base in
1996, a precious life given to Jesus

Saying yes to new life in Jesus;
nothing will ever be the same again.

The Baker family with some of the Zimpeto
Base children in Maputo, late 1990s

Heidi and the Zimpeto base boys in Maputo
ready for Holy Spirit adventures, late 1990s

Reaching the Villages for Jesus

A family ready to be loved

Precious treasures full of life in a remote village

Sharing the gospel on an outreach in the bush

Drilling wells: Clean water saves lives!

Dancing for Jesus in a village church

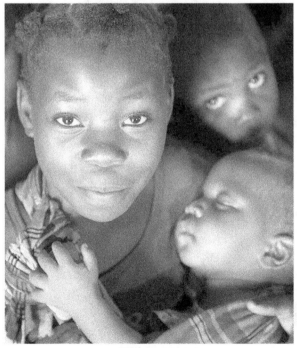

Hope wins

Desperate to see His face

Rejoicing with joy unspeakable and full of glory

Our children adore camping out to share
God's love in villages near and far.

Heidi making new friends in a village
in Northern Mozambique

True worshipper

Little prayer warrior

Our Pemba Center in Northern Mozambique; Home Since 2004

The Pemba base, "Village of Joy," in Northern Mozambique

Community children ready for a celebration lunch feast

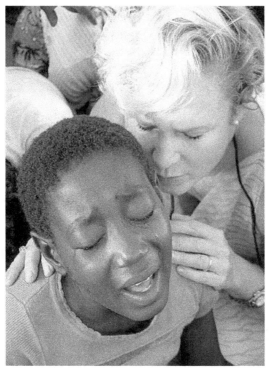

Loving the one

Baptisms in the Indian Ocean—hungry for Jesus!

Worshipping with our Harvest School of Missions
and Mozambican Bible School

Papa Rolland after his first day of flying our new Kodiak!
What a milestone...

Our girls just home from a day of school at
our Pemba Village of Joy School.

Dedicating the new baby house on our Pemba Base

Church on our Pemba Base, worshipping the King of kings

Ready for church and hugs!

Chapter 7

LAVISHLY LOVED

> *How great is the love the Father has lavished on us, that we should be called children of God! And that is what we are!*
>
> —I JOHN 3:I

UNDERSTANDING THAT YOU are a son or a daughter of God and knowing how lavishly the Father loves you is what makes you free to enter your destiny. Only this can give you confidence enough to say yes to the fullness of the call God will put in your heart. If you can catch even a glimpse of how warmly God smiles upon you, you will want to give Him everything for the rest of your life. You will go to the ends of the earth for Him. Whether it means living in the dirt with the poorest of the poor or being salt and light to Harvard elites, we are all called to shine in our own way. God has a special pair of shoes just for you, perfectly suited for your own path. You must learn to wear your own shoes and never put on anyone else's. Walk in your anointing.

Discovering the Father's Heart

I came to faith on an Indian reservation when I was sixteen years old. For my entire life up to that point I had wanted to become a dancer. I practiced for many hours six days a week. The day after I gave my life to Jesus, I was also filled with the Holy Spirit. When He fell upon me, I was filled with so much joy I could not contain it. I was rolling up and down the aisles of my new Pentecostal church, praying in tongues, heedless of everyone around me. At that point it was natural for me to start dancing in His presence. I made it worship. I danced constantly, inside and outside of church—my own Holy Ghost dance.

This new church I found was much freer than the Episcopalian congregation in which I had been raised. But although they allowed a lot more personal expression than I was used to, they were still quite rigid about certain things. For one thing, they were deeply suspicious of dancing. When they noticed I was dancing in worship, it was not long before some of them began to tell me dancing was a sin.

I was determined to please God at any cost. I believed these older and more experienced Christians knew what they were talking about, so I laid my ballet shoes at the altar. I was so tender, so utterly taken by the love of Jesus, that I was willing to give up anything for Him.

After I packed away my toe shoes, I laid down on my face in complete surrender. I have remained in that posture since the day I was saved. Giving up dancing was excruciatingly painful—yet it was also wonderful because I experienced it as a sacrifice of love. Three years later when I was a college student, Jesus gave me back the dance. The campus ministry pastor at Vanguard University asked if anyone had a background in dance and theater. I was shocked by the question since it was a Christian college, but I attended the meeting. The Lord used Dr. Don Baldwin to set me free to dance for Jesus. I started a dance and drama team that ministered around the world, leading thousands to the Lord.

Twenty years later I had a vision. I was on my face sobbing, and the Father came to me with a big smile on His face. I felt indescribable love and acceptance coming from Him. In the vision I had long curly hair with flowers in it, the way I had worn it when I was a teenager. God looked at me—a little blonde hippie flower child—and said He wanted to dance with me.

He picked me up, and we started to dance all around an open field. We leaped and pirouetted, gliding across the green grass. I was exhilarated but also surprised. I had no idea He liked dancing so much, but as we continued He smiled, and I could feel His pleasure. He was simply delighted in me.

I realized that God *likes* me. He does not just like what I can do for Him—He really likes me!

God knows I will obey Him at every moment. That has become easy. When I feel love like this, I will do anything. Our dance was a moment of redemption that spoke directly to my own heart. He gave me back the very thing I had given up for Him, and once again I was completely undone.

Authority Comes From Love

Lavish is an incredibly rich word. It means "over the top, more than you could imagine"—like when we read, "How great is the love the Father has lavished on us, that we should be called children of God!" (1 John 3:1).

No matter how great we are, we do not naturally deserve to be called sons and daughters of God. Even if we achieved top academic honors in school, the highest promotions at our jobs, and every other qualification this world could possibly offer, we would never merit such a gift. Only His free and lavish love gives us the most beautiful title of all— not doctor, not lawyer, not apostle, but son or daughter.

We are the family God went out and found. He was so determined to call us sons and daughters that He suffered on a cross and died. Jesus and His Father are one. Whatever Jesus does, the Father does. They act together, and the cross expresses the unity of their love for us. Jesus died so we could be brothers and sisters to one another. Before that we could not be one family.

I have been beaten up, shot at, and lied about. People have even tried to strangle me. I am not afraid. To this day I can walk boldly into gangs of armed thugs and tell them to stop in the name of Jesus. I expect them to drop their knives. Generally they turn surprisingly nice. Sometimes they look at me and apologize.

Where did this confidence come from? It came from knowing the Father loves me. Because I truly know that I am loved, I am not afraid.

God wants your ministry to flow from the realization that you are a beloved child of God. In that place you don't worry too much about how people see you. You don't worry too much about whether they're nice or mean. You don't even worry about whether they love you or hate you. You don't worry because you're simply going to love them and love Him. This comes from knowing who He is and what He thinks of you. This is what it means to grasp you are a child of God.

But what if we make messy mistakes? What if it turns out we are still flawed people who can be difficult to get along with? Will He keep on loving us then?

We have taken in thousands of children to live with us over the years. One of them was a particular rascal. If he could find something wrong to do, he would do it. He stole everything he could get his hands on. He beat up his brothers and sisters. He was a compulsive liar. He got someone pregnant and denied the child was his. He was angry, bitter, and incredibly inventive in finding new ways to be difficult.

When he was old enough, we gave him a little house. We tried to train him to take care of it. We believed God was going to use his life, but he went on making unbelievable messes in every one of his significant relationships. After a while he ran away, abandoning his house. This was terribly frustrating because we have thousands of children in need of housing. Each home we build is precious.

I asked God what to do about this one. God told me to love him. I responded that I *did* love him—but he never passed at school, failed every course no matter how many we put him through, and cheated constantly. I asked again what God wanted me to do with the boy. Again I felt God say He wanted me to love him. Frustrated, I asked the Lord *how* He wanted me to love him. I sensed the Lord saying He wanted me to give him some time and to pray for him every day and that then God would bring him into His own house.

So that is what I and the other caretakers did. For a long time we could see no progress. Despite everything, this boy was always very charismatic, and after a while he managed to move to the United Kingdom.

Recently, when I was speaking in the United Kingdom, I saw this spiritual son again. At once I was startled to see how powerfully the presence of God was resting on him. When he came up to me, he started weeping and shaking in my arms. In broken English he said, "Thank you, Mama, for not stop loving me."

I started to cry as well and fell to the ground, still holding him in my arms. He was praying hard for God to show up in the meeting. He was blessing me and weeping over me with all his heart.

While we embraced, suddenly I felt God ask me if I would have given my life for this one.

"Yes," I responded. "I would have given my life for this one."

When Jesus gave Himself for us, He was looking forward to the joy set before Him (Heb. 12:2). Our joy in this son was not so much in seeing him graduate from school, though we were very happy when he did. Our joy was seeing him filled with the presence of God. Our joy was seeing him come home to the Father's house and step into the spirit of adoption.

That boy—now a man—knows now who he is. He is a son. He knows better than most that God loves him no matter how many times he might have lied, stolen, beaten up innocents, or committed adultery. He is loved because of the incredible grace of God that comes down to call each of us sons and daughters. None of us deserve it. We simply have it.

Your heavenly Father loves you in the same way. He wants you, no matter what you do or how you fail. This is the love He spoke over us when He sent His Son. It is what Jesus poured out on the cross. It is the thing the church must demonstrate to the world. Love so lavish can never die.

Because of this love, we have become children of God. Even if we do not yet believe it, this is what we truly are (1 John 3:1). We have had children who, for the longest time, would not believe they were truly loved. This particular son had been with us for fourteen years before he finally got it. That is a lot of waiting and a lot of pain. If the Holy Spirit ever touches people in such a way that they realize they are sons or daughters instantly, we ought to celebrate it as a mighty miracle—because sometimes it takes fourteen years.

You are a son or a daughter right now—today. Your real identity is in this truth. It doesn't matter what people do or do not call you. It doesn't matter where you do or do not sit. You are a son. You are a daughter. There is no more precious position to which you might ever aspire.

Loving as Jesus Does

Do you want to be like Jesus? Do you want to look like Him, smell like Him, and feel like Him? We do! We may have a long way to go, but that is our only goal. We want to act like Him and love like Him.

The apostle John tells us that when Christ appears, we will be like Him (1 John 3:2). Every single one of us is created in His image. Even those we seem least able to understand are made in the image of God. Each one has intrinsic value. Each carries divine beauty.

We need to look at people the way Jesus does. He gave Himself so that all would know His lavish love. To show this love is our call. It is the one goal for which we have many different anointings.

This call is not something too difficult for us to understand. We cannot run from it. Our task is to love everyone around us until each one knows what it means to be a child of the living God. We must serve one another until we have all grasped the spirit of adoption. We must see the beauty we bear.

Because we are His sons and daughters, He has promised us He will not leave us as orphans (John 14:18). This is especially important to us because of what God has called us to do in Mozambique with widows and orphans. He told us to love them all and embrace them as family. We keep wondering how this will be possible, but God makes a way.

Because we believe so strongly in the spirit of adoption, we do not call our centers "orphanages." God is faithful to His Word—no one is to remain fatherless. Sometimes when visitors come, we can tell they were expecting to see a lot of misery. They show up and seem surprised that our children are happy. We tell them this is because God did not leave them as orphans. They have been adopted. They have family. They are full of love. In fact, our children are often the ones who minister their Father's heart to the visitors!

Our visitors come from all over the world. Some are pastors. Some are volunteers who own very little themselves.

Others are wealthy and well dressed. Twenty or thirty of our children will come over and gather around one or two of these visitors. Often the children have been playing outside all day, and they will press their dusty little hands right down on the heads of the newcomers and start praying—and they do not have a light touch! Perfect hair will not last long here; sometimes our children will start to braid it. But they bless our visitors with all their hearts. Theirs is a hilarious and very beautiful ministry.

We spend a lot of time hugging the children. We pray God's love over them constantly. Personally I have never seen happier children anywhere else. They are not orphans—and neither are you. Daddy adopted you. He looks you in the eyes and says you are perfect.

We are able to become lovers of God because He already accepts us. We may think we know ourselves, but when we do not accept ourselves, we only prove how little we understand. What a tragedy! The truth is that the God of the universe loves us deeply. We are covered in His blood. That is what allows us to know and love Him. When we understand this fully, we will walk in holiness and be altogether healed.

When you get a revelation of the Father's heart, you will not go around as a grouchy, bitter person, obeying Him grudgingly. You will not be forever complaining about His commands.

All the time people say to me, "I *really* do not want to go to Africa. But I know if I kneel down on the floor right now, He's going to tell me to go to Africa. Can I please just write you a check instead?"

What a funny attitude!

God is *kind*. He may or may not call you to Africa, but if

He does, you will love Africa. We love Africa, Asia, Europe, and everywhere else the Lord has sent us. Wherever He calls you to go, you will go happily. You will be glad to love the ones He gives you to love.

Sometimes people pity us. They say, "You work with the poor. There is malaria, cholera, dysentery. You hang out in the slums. You make such great sacrifices!"

We laugh. None of this seems like any great sacrifice to us. We are glad to give our lives. We are ministers who are filled up with the joy of the Lord; this is our strength. We will never write a newsletter about how miserable it is. It is the most wonderful thing in the world to watch God pour out His love in a garbage dump. Truly, when He is there, it becomes the most glorious cathedral on earth.

John 14:15 says, "If you love me, you will obey what I command." When you love and know that you are loved, obedience is natural. You will find sin hideous. You will be holy simply because you cannot stand the thought of hurting the One you love.

To be a son or daughter of God also means you are royalty. This is the greatest of privileges, but it is also an awesome responsibility. If you are truly thankful to God and want to please Him with all your heart, you must do more than just recognize your own authority. You must use it. He asks you to give love as freely as you have received it— not just to those who deserve it but also to everyone He puts in front of you.

These days I spend a third of my life traveling and speaking in churches and conferences. In the West I have lost track of how many sermons I have heard about how we are sons and daughters of God. I am happy to repeat this message. It is beautiful and true. However, it is vital to realize what Jesus showed us about the way a royal son behaves. The King of kings chose birth in a stable. He knew what it meant to be in the dirt with the poor. He laid His life down. He knew exactly who He was, yet for us He chose to become nothing.

In His kingdom greatness means being the servant of all (Mark 9:35).

Walk in Your Own Shoes

> For we are God's workmanship, created in Christ Jesus to do good works, which God prepared in advance for us to do.
> —EPHESIANS 2:10

Every son and every daughter is unique. Each one has a particular calling from the Lord. Once we have imbibed the lavishness of His love, we will find the greatest possible satisfaction in walking the unique paths He sets. Do not try to copy someone else's calling. It is very difficult to dance ballet while wearing boots. If He gave you ballet shoes, dance ballet; if He gave you lumberjack boots, cut down trees.

I know what it is like to try on the sort of anointing that belongs to someone else. Once at a large conference I was in the ladies' room when I overhead a woman talking about me. "They invited Heidi," she said. "She's probably just going to lie on the floor the whole time."

That comment hurt. "I'm Dr. Baker," I thought. "I have a PhD. I studied for ten years. I have many intelligent things to say." I decided I should make my next message a properly sophisticated one.

I went to the home of the family I was staying with and locked myself in the guestroom. I borrowed all the books in the house and spent the next three hours writing page after page of notes and quotes. Soon I was quite proud of the sermon I had prepared.

I returned to church a little while before I was scheduled to speak in order to pray. As I lay stretched out on the floor, I felt the Lord ask if I wanted to go back.

I knew in my spirit He was asking if I wanted to go back to relying on my education. He would let me try to impress people with my learning if I wanted to.

"No!" I cried out, tears springing to my eyes. "No! I'm sorry!"

When the service started, I stood in front of over a thousand people. Most of them were experienced pastors. I took one step toward the podium and crashed straight to the floor. The Holy Spirit completely unstrung me. As I fell helplessly onto my face, my thick sheaf of carefully prepared notes flew from my hands and scattered all around me on the stage. I began sobbing.

"I cannot go back," I told the audience. "I do not have sophistication. I do not have some snazzy words or notes and quotes. I am just a laid-down lover. All I want to do is love Him." I repented to them for trying to be anything other than myself.

Many ministers are brilliant with their words. They can do amazing things with sermon structure, research, and oratory. They can do all the notes and quotes. That is a wonderful gift—but I cannot preach the way they do because God gave me different gifts.

While I lay there sobbing, the majority of the pastors there fell down under the Holy Spirit all around me. I did not preach anything. Nothing I could have come up with would have done what God chose to do on His own initiative.

On another occasion I tried one more time to prepare myself for speaking with notes and quotes. I headed to a bookstore to get some references but fell down under the weighty glory of God right between the shelves.

On the bookstore floor I had another vision. I felt God telling me to look at my feet, so I glanced down. I was wearing huge clown shoes. They were so ridiculous and so comically oversized that I could not have walked anywhere in them. Then I sensed the Lord speak very clearly that I ought not to wear anyone else's shoes. He desires that each one of His sons and daughters walk in the tailor-made shoes He has for them. There is a specific destiny and anointing for each one. It is as useless to try to be someone else as it is for me to try to walk comfortably in big clown shoes.

I never did get up. Hours later several people carried me up some stairs onto a stage, laid me behind the pulpit, and handed me a microphone. I still did not have a single quote, so I told them all I knew: that they needed to take time to stop before they could go; that they needed to understand rest so they could continue to run and finish strong; that it is in the place of intimacy with Jesus that we find out who He is and who we are in Him.

He is the One who makes us free to be ourselves, and that freedom has a purpose. Each of us has an authority that is unique to us and also a specific field to harvest. To reap the harvest, we need to use the authority He gives us. We need to understand who we are. If we want to bear fruit for Him, we will also step out and take the risk of being the people He truly made us to be—even when it does not look the way others expect.

We had a young woman called Yonnie come to work with us at our Village of Joy in Pemba, Mozambique. All her life Yonnie's parents told her she had to become either a doctor or a lawyer. She chose to be a doctor but never finished medical school. Instead she became a physician's assistant. When she arrived, she was miserable over this situation, but she thought running our medical clinic might give her a new sense of satisfaction. She hated it. She truly wanted to obey her parents and do something great for God, but her heart was not in this or anything else she had found to do. She had pushed herself into a tight box.

One day she got too tired to do it anymore. She came to me and confessed she did not want to run the medical clinic.

I did not have anyone else to run it, but I took a deep breath and told her, "OK, you do not have to run the medical clinic. What do you want to do?"

"I want to be the director of fun!" she said.

I asked her what that would look like.

"I am going to have birthday parties for the children," she told me.

That was a divine idea. Not everyone understands how important it actually is. Some of our children have literally been sold for a loaf of bread in the past. Some used to trade their bodies for one Coca-Cola. We have little girls who were prostitutes by the age of ten and boys who remember being raped every night by the police. When we first find them, these children do not know how to play. They do not have much idea what being loved is like.

Some of these children are working on becoming

doctors and engineers now, but that is not what brings us the greatest joy. Rather, our hearts light up when we see them leaping, laughing, jumping, and playing. We get to watch as God rips the fear and torment out of them and they know they are safe, free, and loved. It is visible on their faces.

That is what Yonnie did. She taught children to play. She was able to change a great many of their lives because of her own newfound freedom. She could not get far in someone else's shoes, but she thrives in the anointing that was made for her.

I think too many Christians try to imitate one another, as if we were meant to become mass-produced robots for God. When we do this, we fail to recognize our uniqueness as the gift of God. The truth is that we need that gift in order to accomplish the visions He gives us.

When I preach, bring home a dying child, or show love to someone who is broken inside, I feel God's pleasure. That is what I am created to do. I used to not want to go anywhere outside Mozambique. My favorite place was the garbage dump, and that was that. It did not matter if I was staying in a five-star hotel—being anywhere outside my corner of Africa made me agitated and discontent. The dirt does not bother me. I am used to having bare holes in the dirt for toilets. I know how not to fall into latrines.

But because God is making me more and more free every day, I have also learned to be happy wherever I go. As long as God sends me, I choose to rejoice. On His errands I get to dream what He dreams. I get to be whatever He calls me to be.

I encourage you to reflect on the calling God has given you. Do not worry about what callings He has given someone else. What is it that you want to do? Who do you want to become? For what do you want to be known? If you have never asked the Holy Spirit to speak to you about these things, I encourage you to spend time doing so now. You will never be happier than when you know the unique destiny His love has prepared for your life.

Whether you believe it or not, the truth is that you are a child of God. Whether you are an engineer, scientist, medical doctor, psychiatrist, nurse, preacher, architect, or housewife, He has lovingly created you to fulfill a unique purpose that will glorify Him. Therefore "whatever you do, do it all for the glory of God" (1 Cor. 10:31). Whether you are called to the poor or to the wealthy, to lonely children on your local street or to the students of Ivy League universities, your destiny is to reflect the Father's light to this world in a way only you can.

If you get it all wrong, He will pick you up, swing you around in His arms, and correct you. He will hug you and put you back on your feet. That is how God behaves toward His children. He will dance with you. He will smile as He gazes on your beautiful face. He will lavish His love on you until it overflows.

God has not left you powerless to fulfill your calling. He has given each of His sons and daughters a sword (Eph. 6:17). You need to know how to wield the sword with both hands. You might be called to lay your life down, but you are mighty in Him. There will be seasons in which to remain low and seasons in which to soar like an eagle. Sometimes He will hide you. Sometimes He will show forth His power through you.

The shoes He made for you will not fit anyone else. Fill them.

Chapter 8

The NEED *for* HUMILITY

> And Mary said: "My soul glorifies the Lord and my spirit rejoices in God my Savior, for he has been mindful of the humble state of his servant. From now on all generations will call me blessed, for the Mighty One has done great things for me—holy is his name. His mercy extends to those who fear him, from generation to generation. He has performed mighty deeds with his arm; he has scattered those who are proud in their inmost thoughts. He has brought down rulers from their thrones but has lifted up the humble. He has filled the hungry with good things but has sent the rich away empty."
>
> —LUKE 1:46–53

THE KING OF glory gave up all He was in heaven to pour out all He is here on earth. God emptied Himself, left heaven, and made Himself vulnerable. The Bible says that "for the joy set before Him" (Heb. 12:2), the Lamb of God endured the price of His mission, which culminated in the scorn of the cross. He left behind streets of gold and all the splendor of heaven.

I believe He gave up knowledge, as well. Do you suppose Jesus came out of the womb knowing everything and said, "Follow Me; I am the Son of God"? I don't think so. The Creator of the universe chose to become completely empty. When He came out of the womb, He needed to be nursed at His mother's breast. He was dependent on her for everything He needed, even His very life. The Son of God had to learn how to walk and how to talk. He had to learn a language. He needed those around Him to teach Him the most basic tools of life in Judea. He became a student. When He did this, He was modeling for us the beauty of dependence.

Our King was born to a young woman in a dirty stable full of domestic animals. It might seem an improper or disgraceful way for a king to be born, but for love's sake God humbled Himself.

Often when we go on outreaches in rural Africa, our village hosts stun us with hospitality. They give us their very best. Frequently this means staying in a one-room mud hut with their children—along with a few chickens and maybe a rooster.

The roosters never seem to know what time it is. I have lost count of the number of times I have laid my head down, ready to fall asleep after a long night of preaching, only to hear a confused rooster, in the pitch dark, suddenly crow right in my ear: "Cock-a-doodle-doo!"

I did not grow up in this kind of environment, but I have come to understand a little about life in the dirt. I understand some of the circumstances into which Jesus was born. When I am drifting off to sleep in a mud hut with two or three children on a rough rope bed next to me, trying to ignore the rooster brushing against my head,

I feel the joy of the Lord. Oftentimes there is not enough grass on the roof. When I look up, I can see the clear African sky, free of city lights, full of stars. I call this my billion-star hotel.

Slowed Down by Weighty Glory

When I spent a week on the floor in Canada without being able to walk or talk, God taught me a profound lesson in dependence. I didn't like being unable to get up and move around as I pleased or to speak or even to go the restroom by myself. My extreme need for other people was uncomfortable and inconvenient. I felt very vulnerable. For seven days I literally could not do anything without some fellow member of the body of Christ being there to pick me up and take me where I needed to be.

During this time I felt the Lord telling me I was always moving, but now was the time to stop, be still, and rest. He just wanted me to lie on the floor and let Him love me. He held me in His weighty glory. He slowed me down so I couldn't move outside His presence. He spoke beautiful words to me and made me still.

It remained uncomfortable to be stuck on the floor with no control over myself, but I replied to Him, "Yes, Lord, I yield to Your will!" Of course, I still wanted to move, but I didn't fight Him. Sometimes I found myself thinking I really wanted a drink, and someone I didn't know would come and bring me a glass of water.

God had captured all my attention. He told me I could do nothing without Him and nothing without His body. He was germinating something powerful, causing my own little heart and vision to expand to a bursting point. I believe He was causing my inability to become His ability. I believe God, by His Holy Spirit, overshadowed me and planted a nation inside me.

How does He do that?

Who can say?

He is God, and He does whatever He likes. He will use anyone, even a little mama like me. God can use anybody who is yielded, who is in love with Him, and who says yes.

Nothing Is Impossible With God

During that conference the Lord spoke to me about birthing hundreds of churches in my nation of Mozambique. It was hard to imagine. I know I am only a little jar of clay, but I felt the Lord saying He was inside me and wanted to break Himself out through me.

Perhaps you are as perplexed as I have been at some of God's promises, wondering how they could possibly come to pass. But remember what happened when the angel of the Lord made the most outrageous and incredible promise to Mary. Despite the impossible nature of that word, Mary chose to believe it. Hers was a simple, childlike faith. "I am the Lord's servant," she said. "May it be to me as You have said" (Luke 1:38).

You too can offer God the same prayer.

The next year I was back at Toronto for another conference. I returned determined to seek God for a fresh word. I surely needed it. The previous year, right after I had heard God mention "hundreds of churches," things had only grown more difficult for us. My husband got cerebral malaria. There was a contract out on my life. (I heard it

went for twenty dollars.) We lost our land and were homeless with more than three hundred children.

I remember trying to sit still and listen to the speakers
at the conference. But this time when the Holy Spirit came,
I ended up standing on my head in the middle of church! I
was literally flipped upside down.

I had just written a song to God that said, "Take me and
use me, bruise me if need be, children are crying, people
are dying. Take me and use me." I had always heard God
would never do anything against my will. People said
nothing He did would ever hurt because "the Holy Spirit
is a gentleman." I am not so sure about that. It is not a
normal desire of mine to stand on my head in front of a
few thousand church people, but that is what happened. I
stayed that way for an hour. Afterward my body was covered in bruises from head to toe.

It got worse. While I was standing on my head, some
prophetic fellow came up to me and said, "Excuse me?"

I wondered why someone would even bother to say
"Excuse me" at that point, but he went on, "God spoke to
me and told me to pour water over you. Is that OK?"

"Go ahead," I told him. Why not?

He emptied a big bottle of water over my legs and feet.
It ran down and soaked my clothes. In the middle of a
crowded conference, I was now standing on my head while
sopping wet. I wondered what my old theology professors
would think about the way I had decided to use my ten
years of academic training.

As I was there stuck on my head, I asked God what all of
it meant. I felt Him say, "I'm turning your ministry upside
down. The apostolic is upside down. It's the lowest place
you can go!"

Just after I returned home from this conference, there was massive flooding in Mozambique. In some places there were almost forty days and nights of rain. Water rushed through and covered a huge swath of the country, including hundreds of towns and villages. Thousands of people died—first from the flooding, then from cholera and other water-borne illnesses, and finally from exposure and starvation.

We had a lot of sleepless nights that month. One of our centers was completely covered in water. The staff had to carry the boys and girls to safety on their shoulders. During the evacuation ten of them were stranded and had to sit out the worst of the flooding on top of trees.

Wherever we had resources, we tried to reach as many flood victims as we could. We drove out into the mud and water until our trucks were being washed away along with the roads. After that we walked. Refugee camps were springing up everywhere. People beyond count had lost their homes. Some foreign aid organizations came, but there were more hungry people than they could deal with.

We began to feed as many as we could. We did our best to feed them natural and spiritual bread and found out the nation was extremely hungry for God. People started coming to Jesus by the hundreds and thousands.

Soon United Nations representatives came and asked us how many of their helicopters we wanted to use. They would lend us five to seven helicopters a day! We sent them out with food and preachers. Thousands of churches were birthed while the floodwaters still stood.

In some places food supernaturally multiplied. Once, a bulk shipping vessel entirely filled with containers of food came without warning and unloaded supplies for us. There was no central plan. It was a terrible time, but the positive fruit also far exceeded anything we knew how to expect.

A Song of Humility

It takes humility to nurture something that is beyond your understanding while counting it all as joy. Mary's response to God's word—the song she sang once she learned what she'd been asked to do—can light our way. It held joy and humility close together. She was undone. She had not sought greatness. Her celebration grew from brokenness. Part of her may have wanted to run from this promise that was too great for comprehension, but instead she said yes.

Her reward was the Son of God.

Mary rejoiced in the Lord, but I think she was also required to give grace and mercy to those who judged her when her condition became clear. Sometimes enduring persecution is the way we glorify God in the midst of the incomprehensible and the miraculous.

We may not have enough strength in us to do this, but Mary shows us how to do it supernaturally. We focus on the One who is altogether lovely. We gaze upon the beauty of the Lord and worship Him alone. Then He will cause supernatural strength to come upon us. He will give us grace to pay the cost with joy. He will empower us to bless those who slander us. Because of Him we are able to show mercy to our enemies.

We also need a holy fear to carry God's promises to full term. Mary sang, "His mercy extends to those who fear him, from generation to generation" (Luke 1:50). I believe the essence of this necessary fear is that we must never seek to take His glory for ourselves. May we always carry

His presence and bear within us the very promises of the Most High God—but may we never, ever touch His glory!

"His mercy extends to those who fear Him"—that is the response we are to have when God comes upon us and gives us prophetic promises. No matter how much we have fasted, sacrificed, or toiled, we cannot boast in what we do. We produce nothing alone. I know that I can do nothing without the Lord and nothing without His body, but if I will lie down and love the One who is worthy—if I will fear Him, trust Him, and have faith in Him—His mercy upon a jar of clay like me will be enough to let me carry some of His glory to a lost and dying world.

We cannot cause anything to be birthed in ourselves. Without Him our efforts produce nothing spectacular, no matter how much we strive. The one thing we can do is respond to the Father's words over our lives. We can position our hearts in humility and hunger. Hunger always delights the heart of God.

People often ask me why we see so many more miracles among the poor than among wealthy, comfortable westerners. The answer is simple: The poor know they are in need. They know what it is to be desperate and hungry, and they turn that desperation and hunger toward Him. They stay desperate. They stay hungry. God lifts up the humble, and He fills the hungry with good things (Luke 1:52–53).

> Blessed are those who hunger and thirst for righteousness, for they will be filled.
>
> —Matthew 5:6

Chapter 9

DON'T GIVE UP!

> *When Elizabeth heard Mary's greeting, the baby leaped in
> her womb, and Elizabeth was filled with the Holy Spirit. In
> a loud voice she exclaimed: "Blessed are you among women,
> and blessed is the child you will bear! But why am I so
> favored, that the mother of my Lord should come to me? As
> soon as the sound of your greeting reached my ears, the baby
> in my womb leaped for joy. Blessed is she who has believed
> that what the Lord has said to her will be accomplished!"*
>
> —LUKE 1:41–45

WHEN GOD PLACES a promise inside us, we have
to decide to nurture it and believe that it will be
accomplished. Every word God has ever given me required
me to be patient and tenacious in walking it out. I have had
to make choices and decisions that align with His promises. Saying yes to Him is not something I can do once and
then forget about it. I have to live out that yes every day of
my life. I have to keep feeding what grows in me.

When the Lord told me I would be a minister, I did not

wake up overseas one day in a brand-new church. I had to buy my ticket, get on a plane, and go preach in the slums. When the Lord told me I would get a graduate degree, no one mailed it to me. I had to apply, study for four years, write a thesis, and take many difficult exams.

Feed Your Baby Good Food

Walking out the promises of God means making practical decisions. Mary received a supernatural promise, but she still had to care for her baby. The baby growing inside her needed her loving care in order to thrive. To begin with, she needed to rest, eat well, and take care of herself.

If a mother wants a healthy baby, she eats what is good for her and for her child. Likewise, we have to be careful not to kill or damage our promises with bad "food"— negative attitudes, criticism, backbiting, unbelief, or agitation. These things will not do your "baby" good. We need to nurture that which God puts inside us with the right kind of food.

Most of all we all need to spend time in the secret place. We are nourished by prayer, by Scripture, and by the body of Christ. There may also be more specific food your baby needs. For example, if God has called you to be a healing evangelist, you may need to read about great healing evangelists of the past. You may need to find a mentor with a particular gift for healing. You may need to move to a place where you can learn more and practice.

Whatever it takes, eat the food that will make your baby grow.

Press Into the Promise

For many years I longed to witness healing miracles—for the blind to see, the deaf to hear, the dumb to speak, and the cripples to walk. I was living in the slums and working with the poorest people I could find, so I saw these kinds of afflictions often. My heart was continually broken for them.

Eventually I received a promise from the Lord that the blind *would* see and my nation *would* be transformed. For a year after this I prayed for every single blind person I found.

Not one of them saw.

But I did not give up. I knew I had been overshadowed for this purpose. I had faith. So did my husband and my children. I kept looking for more and more blind people. I would ask for them to come forward at every meeting. If I saw one by the road, I would leap out of my truck and lay my hands on them. Almost everyone I prayed for got saved, but for the longest time no one gained vision.

And then one day it began to happen.

I was in a dark little mud-hut church in central Mozambique, laying my hands on an old blind lady. Her eyes were clouded, the irises and pupils totally white. Suddenly, as I was praying for her, she fell down on the dirt floor. I watched her eyes go from white to gray and then to dark, shiny brown. After all the years of hoping, crying, and trying, I witnessed what I had waited for. The woman could see!

Delighted beyond words, I asked her, "What's your name?"

She said, "Mama Aida."

"My name is Mama Aida too!" I exclaimed. (The Portuguese version of the name *Heidi* is *Aida*, so this is what I am called at home in Mozambique.) There were about forty people in church. Soon everybody started yelling and screaming, "Mama Aida can see!"

That night we went to another mud-hut church in a different village. They brought in an elderly woman who had been blind since she was eight years old. I prayed for her, and I wept as I held her. Then she interrupted me, screaming, "You are wearing a black shirt!"

Her eyes were opened.

We went outside, and a crowd started to gather around her. Very soon the village became filled with yelling and running and dancing. As it so happened, her name was Mama Aida too! This was very strange. For the second day in a row a new village rang with cries of "Mama Aida can see! Mama Aida can see!"

The day after this we went to yet a third village in a place called Chimou. This time a large crowd came. As usual, after preaching I asked them to bring me the blind, deaf, and disabled. A young boy dressed in rags led a blind woman to me through the crowd. She was elderly, like the two women before.

We prayed. The presence of God came. The woman fell down as she was touched by the Spirit and began to cry, "I can see! I can see!"

As before the crowd grew loud and excited. The news spread as quickly as people could shout. By now I was almost afraid to ask her what her name was.

"Aida," she said.

In three days this was the third blind lady with the same name as mine to receive her sight!

When I asked Jesus what this meant, I thought He would say something complimentary. Perhaps He would tell me I was coming into my healing anointing. Perhaps I had received the mantle of some famous and anointed healing evangelist—a Kathryn Kuhlman or an Aimee Semple McPherson.

What I actually felt from the Lord shocked me. I felt Him say I was blind!

I did not enjoy hearing that. Stunned, I told God, "But I am a minister! I've been sharing about Jesus since I was sixteen, and I live with the poor!"

Twice more I sensed the Lord tell me I was blind.

I fell apart. I threw my hands over my face and sobbed. I begged God to open my eyes and let me see.

He did. In my spirit I suddenly saw the Western and the Eastern bride of Christ—countless outwardly rich churches that are, in truth, badly malnourished. I saw the Father's many, many children in affluent nations trying to live on a few stray crumbs from His table each day. Though they are called to eat their fill from heavenly realms of glory, they don't realize what they have. An incredible feast is laid out for them, yet they remain on the edge of starvation. I saw people clothed wealthily on the outside yet spiritually dressed in rags. I saw a secret multitude of the hungry, poor, and naked.

I believe Jesus was asking, "Won't you love them too?"

Continue to Say Yes

I didn't know exactly what this meant for my own life, but not long after this the Lord again overshadowed me. He spoke to me about traveling.

For eighteen years I had barely done any speaking in the West. I was happy to be hidden away in slums and garbage dumps, learning about the kingdom from drug addicts and poor children. To be honest, I didn't much care for most of the Western church. All I wanted to do was be with the poor—to sit with them, hug them, and make friends with them. I was content to live with my boys and girls and bring more home from the streets every week. I did not want to be an itinerant minister. I had no ambition to speak at conferences.

One day, not long after the healing of the three Mama Aidas, I was lying in my backyard, worshipping. Some of the children had their hands on me in prayer. As they prayed, I heard the Lord tell me I was to give one-third of my time to ministering in first world nations.

I started crying. I did not want to go. I could hardly imagine leaving my children for even a third of my time. Then I sensed the Lord reminding me of John 14:15: "If you love me, you will obey what I command."

"Lord," I wept, "whatever You want, I will do."

Later that day I opened my computer and found my inbox full of recent e-mails inviting me to minister in many different countries, some of which I had never been to. All of them were affluent nations.

It had been a long while since I had worked with anyone except the poorest of the poor. I had not ministered in the Western world for many years. The only American church in which I had spent any significant amount of time was in Fairbanks, Alaska. I had gone there to rest and recover one winter when I became so sick that I was bedridden for four months. Otherwise I had more or less refused to look at the wealthier churches of the world. Now the Lord was opening my eyes and showing me how He wanted to feed fresh bread from heaven to westerners and easterners of all kinds. He wanted to put salve on their eyes too so they could see clearly.

I began to travel for one-third of the year. I was obedient, but for a long time I was not joyful about it. I often said I hated conferences. When I left Mozambique, I missed my children every moment of every day. While I sat in pleasant hotels, I longed to be with the poor in the dirt. I was constantly homesick.

One day the Lord gently rebuked me. He told me He was glad I obeyed, but He also wanted me to be joyful in the work. This greatly impacted my heart.

I was in the Ukraine when the Lord began to teach me how to do what He was asking. I felt He told me to "see the one in front of me." At that moment I was holding a Ukrainian lady in my arms, and suddenly, to my amazement, I felt the very same love for that woman as I did for my Mozambican children.

Soon after that I was hugging and praying for an Israeli youth in Jerusalem. All at once I felt the deep weight of God's affection for the youth's nation and people. I found myself thinking that if I had to, I would gladly take a bullet for them. Right there I literally became willing to lay my life down for this young Jewish man.

More and more each day I started to really see the one God was placing in front of me, and then the next, and the next after that. God taught me to do this while I was in richer nations, just as I had learned to do it in poorer ones. From then on I started to find joy in my travels.

Since then I have flown over two million miles. I have gotten used to sleeping in different hotel rooms every night and changing time zones every few days. When God opened my eyes, I saw that the prosperous Western and

Eastern parts of the world are full of hungry, desperate people too. Because of what He showed me, I said yes to getting on an endless succession of planes. I said yes to leaving my children behind over and over again. For the joy that is set before me, I say yes every day to the cost of the promises God is birthing through me.

I can also truthfully say that it has become one of my greatest joys to travel around the world, even though not long ago it felt like one of my greatest sacrifices. It is a privilege for me to see people all over the earth yielding their lives to Jesus on the altar and saying, "I will go, no matter what the cost! I will run into my destiny and carry God's love to this lost and dying world!"

No Matter What It Looks Like

Mary had to wait nine months for her promise to be birthed. Sometimes we must wait years to see what the Lord has spoken come to pass. During those nine months Mary was carrying her promise alone. Others were interceding in the temple, but no one else had her baby inside their womb; no one else literally felt the weight of that baby each day. Mary had to go on a long journey to Bethlehem, and after being turned away from every decent room in the city, she had to wait in a stable to birth her baby. It was dark, there were animals around, it did not smell very pleasant, and only Joseph was there to help her. And then there was the pain of the labor itself. This was not a very glamorous way to see the fulfillment of her promise.

There will be moments when we feel the weight of the promises God has placed inside of us, but we see nothing. We only experience a long journey and a dusty, stinky stable. Maybe no one is cheering us on or affirming our faith; we may even feel embarrassed in the presence of others. When I was praying for blind person after blind person with not one person healed, I could have looked at my circumstances and felt ashamed or confused, especially in front of my friends. I could have given up hope and stopped praying, but I would have missed the breakthrough.

In these waiting seasons we choose to fix our eyes on the One who is worthy, to fix our eyes on Him and take our eyes off of the circumstances that are shaking and breaking and difficult and fix our eyes on the One who is glorious. It matters how we look at things; it matters what we carry; it matters how we see the world. It matters that we focus on the One who is worthy and do not focus on what we haven't seen yet. You have a choice in how you look at things. You have a choice how you see things. Focus on His beautiful face no matter what is going on around you, and keep believing for every promise He has placed in your heart.

Chapter 10

BELIEVE *for the* IMPOSSIBLE

"How will this be," Mary asked the angel, "since I am a virgin?"

The angel answered, "The Holy Spirit will come on you,
and the power of the Most High will overshadow you.
So the holy one to be born will be called the Son of God.
Even Elizabeth your relative is going to have a child in
her old age, and she who was said to be barren is in her
sixth month. For no word from God will ever fail."

"I am the Lord's servant," Mary answered.
"May it be to me as you have said."

Then the angel left her.

—LUKE 1:34–38

T HE FIRST THING Mary said when she heard her promise was, "How will this be, since I am a virgin?" There was no natural way for her promise to come to pass. Jewish Scripture gave her no reference point for what was happening. It must have seemed utterly impossible.

This is often how our promises from the Lord look: completely and utterly impossible! If your promise does not seem impossible, it is likely not from God.

What has God breathed over you? What do your promises look like? If you can produce it by your own effort and ability, it would not need to be supernatural. It has to be supernatural to be God. That is who He is—He is supernatural love manifested. By yourself you cannot produce what He wants to birth in you and through you. God is not after spectacular abilities. He is after given hearts and yielded lives.

Birthing the Supernatural

Naturally speaking, I am completely wrong for the kind of work I do. I am a woman from Laguna Beach, which is a prosperous part of California. For Mozambique I am the wrong color and gender, from the wrong socioeconomic background, with the wrong educational background.

Once I told God how wrong I thought I was. I felt Him say that was precisely what would allow Him to birth something *supernatural* through me.

God makes us right for the tasks He asks of us. He is after those who simply remain willing to give all that they are, people who long for full possession by the Holy Spirit.

When the Lord called us to the Makua tribe in Mozambique, there was nothing we could do to make the tribe love Jesus. We could not come up with any kind of realistic plan to make it happen. At first it seemed as if they did not want to know Jesus. That might have been discouraging to us, but we believed God had declared this was their time of visitation. We knew they would meet Him and know Him because of what He alone would do.

A little while before we moved to the northern city of Pemba, Rolland flew us up there in our little six-seat bush plane for a visit. We wanted to see where the Lord had asked us to move. As we explored Pemba and the surrounding areas for the first time, we found ourselves trying to get over the shock of being told to go to yet another piece of dirt in the middle of nowhere and start over from nothing. There was little business. Electricity and water were sporadic. There was no Internet access, which was hugely challenging because we handle most of our administration via e-mail. We did not have the financial resources to start a new base. We had no place to live.

Pemba is on the ocean and incredibly beautiful, though most of the people are extremely poor. This beauty might have seemed like a good thing to most people, but when I saw how lovely it was, I almost decided I could not live there. For the longest time my identity had been in slums, garbage dumps, and back alleys. I thought I would be serving God better if I stayed in the ugly places where no one else wanted to go. When I said this to the Lord, I am sure I heard Him laugh at me. He reminded me that people who live in beautiful places can be lost and hungry too.

The first time I shared the gospel in Pemba was in front of a local craft shop. I think the only reason anyone stayed to listen was that they hoped to sell me some of their wares. It didn't matter. God was faithful. After sharing about the life, death, and resurrection of Jesus Christ, we had the very first members of our northern congregation—Mohammed, Omar, Ishmael, and Amadi. These and a number of others gave their lives to the Lord Jesus then and there.

Soon after that we decided to try a bigger outreach on the outskirts of Pemba. As evening fell, we got our sound system set up, with our little generator rumbling away to power it. A few of our Mozambican friends that had come up with us from the south started playing the drums and singing.

A crowd showed up, but for a long time nothing worked very well. A well-known preacher had come to visit us and was trying his best to deliver a rousing sermon. No one seemed to be paying much attention. Here and there fights were breaking out. After a while some people began throwing sand and rocks at us. The service was quickly turning dangerous. As the situation grew worse and worse, God reminded me of what He had said: *Go and get my Makua bride.*

As I cried out to the Lord, asking Him what I should do, I felt He was leading me to give an altar call for the demonized. Given this crowd—most of whom were of another faith, mixed with the local traditions of witchcraft—that did not sound like a good plan to me. I did it anyway. In my experience, when the Holy Spirit overshadows you, you do strange things.

I asked the crowd if they would like to see the power of God, and then I invited everyone who suffered from demonic afflictions to come to the front.

To my surprise about thirty people came forward immediately. As they made their way through the crowd, they started twitching, growling, and manifesting demon spirits. We were not in a church building. We all stood on broken pieces of cement and dirt. I was not sure what to do. I had prayed for individuals with demons before, but I had never seen anyone give an altar call for the demonized.

Asking God for help, I backed up a little bit from the line of demonized people and watched them. They were manifesting their possession. It was ugly. They were not Christians, but they all knew they had demons, and they truly wanted to get rid of them.

Everyone in that part of Africa knows something about evil spirits. The crowd was interested now. They looked on eagerly.

Finally I did the only thing that seemed obvious. Loudly I commanded all the demons to go in Jesus's name. All thirty people fell down immediately. Wherever they fell, they lay stuck to the cement. They could not do anything.

I went down the line and picked them up one by one, asking each of them what happened. All that any of them could tell me was that they were feeling much better. All but two had stopped manifesting. I told those two to wait at one side of the line so I could pray for them again. At a second prayer those two dropped to the pavement again. Every person who had come forward for deliverance was now free.

I then asked the crowd, "Who wants Jesus?"

Many cried, "We do!" Everyone knelt down in the dirt and prayed to receive Him. That became the location of our first church in Cabo Delgado Province.

Over the next two and a half years we planted two hundred more churches among the Makua. At the time of this writing, ten years later, more than two thousand churches have sprung up in Cabo Delgado.

Get a Bigger Boat

A few years ago the Lord stirred me up to reach the most isolated people in Cabo Delgado—the ones living in scattered coastal villages along the region's many islands and inlets. Most are unreachable by road. They had never heard the gospel. As soon as I learned about them, I began to intercede for them daily, pondering how I might get to them.

Later I was preaching in New Zealand and decided to go and buy a good outdoor backpack for bush outreaches. As I walked into the sports store, I noticed a brightly colored kayak in the window. An exciting idea hit me: What if I could simply paddle to those coastal villages?

I bought the kayak on the spot. You have to start somewhere.

When the kayak arrived in Mozambique, I tried to row to the nearest of the coastal villages dotting Pemba's bay. I made it from one beach to the next one over before I got too tired to keep going. I wondered if I needed to start doing some serious weight training.

I was getting ready to try again, but when I prayed over the journey, I felt God telling me to wait until we could buy a bigger boat. Good plan! We did some research. Soon Iris Global was able to purchase a modest twenty-six-foot vessel.

The first place we took it was a village called Londo. We anchored offshore and jumped into the dinghy. Our dinghy was old and battered and had holes patched over with duct tape, but it was strong enough to get us to the beach.

When Pastor Jose, Dilo, and I arrived at the village, we asked who knew the chief. In Mozambique you do not enter a village without getting permission from the chief.

They said he was on a long fishing trip, but that the man next in charge would talk to us. We hiked up a muddy hill and found this person in an old carpenter's shed. It looked like the sort of place Jesus would have enjoyed.

The man gave us permission to speak to the villagers, who slowly gathered around us as we started to sing hymns in Makua. When most of the village had arrived, we told them about the man named Jesus who healed the sick, cast out evil spirits, and loved them without condition. They said they would like to meet Him. In fact, they wanted us to bring Jesus along on our boat next time we visited.

I shared how Jesus had died to take away their sins and had then risen from the dead. I told them that now Jesus lived inside my heart, in the hearts of Jose and Dilo, and in everyone who was willing to believe.

We played an audio recording of the Gospel of John read in Makua for the villagers. They asked many questions. Before the sun went down, they all invited Jesus to live in their hearts.

Adults and children followed me and my friends back to the shore. They asked us to come back as soon as we could to tell them more.

On our way home one of the boat's engines blew up. We made it home at a crawl, but it took six weeks, a parts shipment from Canada, and a Filipino mechanic to get the engine running again.

When we finally came back, the villagers saw the boat approaching in the distance. They lined up on the shore, singing and dancing. They were quoting Scriptures and singing songs they had memorized from the solar-powered audio Bibles we had left them. After that we returned to the village of Londo as often as we could.

One night a fierce storm rose up just as we were arriving. We put out in our dinghy and got tossed everywhere by the surf. Before we made it to the shore, we were scared for our lives. We were sopping wet. As usual the villagers were waiting for us on the sand. They were especially excited to see us this time. They wanted to show me my new home. They had made me a fabulous new mud hut on a hill near the church and school we had helped them build.

Their gift was overwhelming. I was laughing and hugging them when I got a call from the boat captain. He was shouting something about the boat sinking.

"No! Not now!" I yelled into the radio. I was busy enjoying my hut.

"You might not want to hear it, but we're sinking!" the captain yelled back.

There was no choice but for a rescue boat to come from Pemba and pick us up. Unfortunately our captain was inexperienced, and the rescue boat's captain was drunk. Our captain shot his single emergency flare sideways into the water. It took the rescuers hours to find our vessel. The weather was worsening, and their crew was infuriated. They picked up the people who were on our sinking boat and left me, Jose, Dilo, and Mario behind. They were in no mood to hunt for us on shore.

The villagers shrugged and built us a fire. I laughed to myself while thinking of the apostle Paul's trials. Stoned? Check. Beaten? Check. Jailed? Check. Hungry and cold? Check. Shipwrecked. Check!

Remembering Acts 28, I said a quick prayer to bind any serpents around the fire in Jesus's name.

Before going to bed, I climbed the biggest termite hill in the village, hoping to find cell phone reception from across the bay in Pemba. I got one bar. In the few minutes before my battery died, I texted a team of intercessors at our base, asking for prayer for a miracle. This is the most critical kind of support there is. If your dreams are from God, they will always need intercession. Praying people, like midwives, help birth the miraculous promises in your life. They will make the obstacles before you more bearable.

I went to sleep in one room of my mud hut, with Jose, Dilo, and Mario in the other. Around three o'clock in the morning, I woke up to horrifying screams. I ran out of my room to find my three brothers covered in fire ants. I should have bound those too.

The village had no electricity, and our flashlights were dead. I took them outside and tried to wipe all the fire ants from their swelling arms and legs by the moonlight. They were in absolute agony.

Maybe we were naïve to try sleeping again after that.

Before the first cock crowed, the whole village surrounded our hut in predawn darkness. They started singing. They were used to getting up that early, and now they were excited for us to come and dedicate their new church.

We were exhausted beyond belief. We got up and stumbled toward the new church while the villagers danced around us. We were too tired even to stop at the latrine. Blurry-eyed and covered in welts from the fire ants, we dedicated the church and the school to Jesus with all the strength and enthusiasm we had. Dilo, Jose, and I preached until we were sure we had shared everything the Lord gave us. By then the morning was bright. It was already getting hot. We gave up on sleep, deciding we should try to make our way back to Pemba instead.

The drunken captain who had retrieved our team the

night before never came back for us. We borrowed a local canoe and paddled back to our half-submerged boat. We hoped to use the radio, but the engines were underwater and the electronics were fried. We had to go back to shore and swap the canoe for our battered dinghy. Mario fired up the dinghy's tiny engine. Knowing it would be a long trip, we headed out for Pemba across the open bay.

As it turned out, we had made a bad mistake. The dinghy really did leak. Soon we were knee-deep in water. We thought we were prepared—Dilo, Jose, Mario, and I were all wearing life jackets with whistles and bottles of fresh water—but as the water kept rising, we realized we were all in serious trouble. Life vests would not save us if we were swept out to sea. In earnest now, we prayed for God to send a rescuer.

Pastor Jose's wife was nine months pregnant then. For the last ten years Jose had prayed for a baby. His wife, Albertina, had been barren, but the year before we had all fasted for her, and now her baby was about to be born. She had almost carried her promise to full term. Knee-deep in rising water, Jose cried out, "I just want to see my baby born!"

Jose could not swim. Going on our boat always made him nervous. He went anyway. He wanted to tell everyone he possibly could about the gospel. He said he would do anything for Jesus. Now he was getting to prove it.

Dilo, my adopted son whom I had picked up from the streets years before, was dreaming about food. He went on and on about how starving he was.

Mario, our assistant skipper, had no dreams to discuss.

One of the visions God had given me about my life was that I would preach the gospel in universities around the world. I pondered this dream while the dinghy was sinking.

I had been scheduled to fly to Oxford, England, to speak at an event called Love Oxford the next day.

How would I give birth to my promise?

We saw a small vessel in the distance. As it came closer, we saw it was an ancient-looking fishing boat covered in bird feces. We whistled madly and flailed our arms. It came to us crewed by an old man. He offered to take us back to Pemba—for an exorbitant fee. He was quite the haggler.

I was furious that he would try to take advantage of us with the water reaching our waists. I told him I would never pay him so much. He promptly revved up his engine, happy to leave us there.

My brothers started laughing and crying. They wailed and prayed aloud for God to give me a brain. I realized I needed to call our rescuer back and give him whatever he wanted. I would pay any price to see God's promises birthed in our lives—to bring the love of Jesus to the most hidden people groups, to the top universities, to the lost, the broken, and the dying. I would pay anything to see a mighty movement of radical, laid-down lovers released into every corner of the earth. I supposed I could pay this price too.

After agreeing to hand over a small fortune, we climbed into the fisherman's boat and tried to find a spot to sit down. There was not much room in that dilapidated hull, but to us it was simply amazing.

We left the dinghy behind, never to be seen again. After we had gone a very short distance, however, the engine on this fishing boat blew up.

We fell on our faces laughing. Then we cried more.

Our rescuer told us his engine had never had any

problems before. Therefore he had no oars. We told him we understood. We were quite certain it had to do with us.

The waves started pushing the fisherman's powerless boat toward a cluster of jagged black rocks sticking out from the water. It looked like another shipwreck was about to happen. We prayed intensely in the Spirit. We prayed for our lives and for the miraculous promises God had placed within us. I had to go and preach at Oxford. Pastor Jose had to see his baby being born. Dilo had to eat. Mario just needed to care.

You Never Know What God Will Do

Everything looked lost once again, when in the distance we spotted another local wooden fishing boat. It was just big enough for six people. We blew our whistles furiously. The fishermen paddled over.

The first thing I noticed was that the fishermen were naked. They had not expected to find anyone else on the ocean that day.

Covering my eyes, I asked what a rescue would cost.

"Nothing!" they laughed. "You're going to die if we don't rescue you!"

Right away one of them jumped into the ocean and started heading for the shore. He was a powerful swimmer, but at first I had no idea why he had gone into the water. As he was swimming to shore, another fisherman helped our previous rescuer to safety.

The fisherman who jumped off the boat came back swimming with shorts for himself and the other five fishermen. They covered up and helped us onto their boat. In my life I have been honored in many ways. I have been put in seven-star hotels. I have been taken to extraordinary banquets. On occasion I have flown in private planes and helicopters. However, I had never been honored as much as this.

Jose, the one who could not swim, fell into the ocean while crossing over. For a few moments he bobbed up and down in his orange life jacket screaming. Our new friends fished him out of the water. As he flopped down between the benches, intensely relieved to be alive, I noticed that the bottom of the boat was covered with fish. Then the Lord spoke to me from Ezekiel 47 about the price of the harvest and the vast numbers of fish yet to be caught.

There were now five extra people in a six-man boat. Our boat rocked and keeled to one side in the choppy water, threatening to capsize us. Just when we thought we were going to go under, we heard the six men chanting loudly together. They were pulling up a ragged sail: "Ho, ho, ho!"

The sail went up. We caught the wind. It pulled us upright, and we started to skim speedily across the bay. The day was ending. While we raced homeward, I saw what seemed like the most glorious sunset I had ever witnessed in my life—purple, orange, pink, and red, all blazing with the most magnificent intensity.

When we were nearly back to our side of the bay, I remembered I had a copy of the New Testament in my waist pack.

I also remembered the day when the local representative of a large Bible society explained to me they wanted to donate thirty thousand New Testament books to Iris Global. These Bibles came with conditions. Although I, a woman, was one of the senior leaders of the movement, they did not want any of their New Testaments to be received by a woman. Only Mozambican men were to receive them.

At first I was offended. Then the Holy Spirit reminded me there were hundreds of men in our region working with Iris who were ready to receive this priceless gift and to distribute it to others. That very day I called over one hundred men to our office to receive the first of these New Testaments. I waited on the sidelines while they took them—but in the end, one of the men made sure to give me a few extra copies as he left. I still had the last one of these with me.

If you want to birth the miraculous, you cannot afford to waste time getting offended. Offense stops you carrying the promise to full term, and you really never know what God plans to do with a situation that offends you at first.

When we reached our side of the bay, I took out this little New Testament and read John 3:16 to my rescuers. I was surprised to discover one of the fishermen knew how to read. I left the book with him. All six men received the Lord Jesus as their Savior on the shore before we said good-bye.

We had arrived on dry land close to home, but we had not birthed all our promises just yet. We had to walk our way through one of Pemba's outlying villages. We recalled that this village was notorious for banditry. Normally we would never go there after dark. We were bone-weary and terrified.

I am blonde and fair-skinned. I do not blend into African villages easily, particularly while wearing a bright orange life jacket. Once again we were praying with our hearts in our throats, fearing robbery or worse.

We made it to the road without incident, but then the

first vehicle we saw stopped beside us. It was all black with darkened windows. A window rolled down. Rough-looking men inside demanded to speak with us. This car belonged to one of the bandit chiefs.

My son Dilo had a few uncooked fish with him. After dreaming of food all day, he had purchased them from our fishermen rescuers before we parted ways. When the bandits smelled the raw fish, they decided we all stank too much to bother with. They told us to keep moving.

We kept walking in the dark, hoping to hitch a safer ride. Finally a truck stopped for us. The driver told us we could hop in the back. We bumped down the dusty road and, at long last, arrived home. We were dropped off at the gates of the Iris center we call the Village of Joy.

When they saw us, our children ran down the hill, dancing and weeping. We had been out of touch for more than a day. No one was sure what had happened to us. My dear friend Mary-Ann had already started to receive e-mails asking if I was alive. The children were scared we had been lost at sea.

The four of us fell in the dirt, rejoicing under the children's hugs. We really did feel like God had saved our lives.

A Hard-Won Harvest

I arrived home wet, hungry, and completely exhausted. The first thing I had to do was pack for my trip to Oxford.

The following day I flew to Johannesburg, the capital of South Africa, and then got in line for my next flight to England. I found out my seat was in the middle row in the very back of the plane. I was still far from properly rested. The thought of being stuck between three other passengers for the nine-hour flight made me want to cry. I asked the flight agents if I could possibly wait to board the plane until the last moment, in case any aisle seats became available. I was flying on an airline I did not normally use. I did not expect much favor. I waited, praying, as the other passengers boarded, feeling frayed and stretched to my limit.

Just before they closed the doors, they called me to the gate desk. The attendant smiled and said, "We have an aisle seat for you. It's in first class."

I burst into tears.

After I reached my seat, they gave me a set of pajamas. I had never experienced such an incredibly comfortable flight before in my life. I slept all the way to London.

I arrived at Oxford in traditional British weather—cold, heavy rain. The event was outdoors. As we worshipped together, the presence of God seemed to so fill the outdoor area that no one paid any attention to the downpour. Under their umbrellas I saw countless men and women bowing their knees. Many made commitments to carry their own miraculous promises to full term, no matter the cost. Some fell face down in the mud, floored under the weight of God's presence.

All at once everything I had been through over the last several days felt utterly worthwhile.

Cast Your Bread Upon the Waters

After that shipwreck I asked the Lord what we should do next to reach the coast settlements. Our experience with boating so far had been fruitful, even spectacular, but also tragically short.

Again I felt the Lord saying, "Get a bigger boat!"

A friend of mine named Mattheus van der Steen, from Holland, heard I was praying for a bigger vessel. He found a yacht on the market for less than 10 percent of its original worth. It had previously belonged to the king of Spain. Iris Global purchased it, and nearly a hundred volunteers worked for over a year to restore it. We ripped out the king's quarters and put in bunk beds so we could transport more team members on outreach. At its launch we named it *Iris Compassion.*

The first time we took the *Iris Compassion* on outreach, we brought a large team of worshippers and intercessors, including as many children as we could safely fit aboard. The children knew it was their boat because they belong to the King!

We decided to let the captain pray about where to take us on the first voyage. He knew of a village we had never visited before and took us there while we worshipped on the sunny deck.

As usual we intended to go and find the chief before doing anything else. But before we could go exploring, we saw a little boat motoring in from the open bay. Those aboard waved as they headed past us toward the village. We asked them to stop for a moment so we could throw them a big bag of fresh bread. We tossed it to their boat, but it fell short, landing in the water. The plastic was well sealed, though, and the bread stayed afloat.

As they came around to pick up the bread, the Lord reminded me of the scripture, "Cast your bread upon the waters, for you will find it after many days" (Eccles. 11:1, esv). As they got closer, I asked them in their language if they knew where the local chief was. The man in the middle looked up and said, "I am the chief." Right away he offered to take me on a tour of his village.

At that moment the engine on the chief's boat choked, sputtered, and died. (We seem to have quite the anointing for engines at Iris Global!) We were happy to help and sent our mechanic to examine the problem. They needed a specific kind of spark plug that we happened to have on board. I asked our captain to give them one. He looked at me quite strangely. Spare parts can be very hard to come by in Mozambique, and we were likely to need everything we had brought with us to keep the *Iris Compassion* going, but I insisted.

If we are to carry our promises to full term, we need to help others do the same. If we want to arrive at our intended destinations, we must help others cross the water. We all have things that our brothers and sisters need in order to fulfill their own destinies. We are called to share and provide those things.

After we got the chief's boat running, Jacinto, Dilo, and I decided to go the rest of the way with the chief. We left the intercessors on our boat to keep praying and worshipping.

We landed on a wide, muddy delta, stretching out into salt flats. The village was several miles away. It grew hotter as we walked under the midday sun, past beds of salt and one family of curious baboons. When we reached the village, we found its people fasting without water and praying for God to bless their lives. They were devout in another faith.

In thirty-seven years of preaching I think I have yet to see a warmer welcome than the one we received that day. Family after family came out of their huts to hug and greet us. The chief pulled out his best plastic chairs and set them out for us under a mango tree. He called out the king and queen of the village, the teachers, and the elders. All of the children decided to show up too and see what we were up to. When hundreds had gathered, the chief asked us why we had come.

I started with John 3:16: "For God so loved the world that he gave his one and only Son, that whoever believes in him shall not perish but have eternal life." After I shared these simple words from the Bible and spoke about what they meant, the king, queen, chief, elders, children, teachers, and everyone who could hear us bowed their heads and received Jesus as Lord and Savior. All those present gave themselves to Jesus without question.

The chief offered us the best piece of land available to build a church. Afterward he even called up several distant friends with motorcycles to come in and give us a ride back. We sped past the baboons, boarded our ship, and cruised back to Pemba just in time for our mission school and Bible school graduation ceremony; six hundred students representing thirty different nations had spent the last several months studying with us. From this group we formed twenty teams to minister all around the world. Others returned to their home cities and villages, ready and willing—we hoped—simply to stop for the one.

We are still eagerly waiting to see more of this vision come to pass. I expect God to give Iris a freighter ship next!

A Little Kayak to the King's Yacht

Sometimes we feel foolish dreaming the sorts of dreams God puts in our hearts. Our truest dreams always look too big for us. We may be afraid of how bizarre we will look trying to achieve them. We might start out trying to paddle a kayak alone to islands many miles away only to find the task is much harder than we ever knew. Nonetheless, we can be confident that He who began a good work in us will bring it to completion (Phil. 1:6).

Scripture says Paul prayed for the church to have patience and endurance (Col. 1:11). Sometimes we give up too quickly. I might have given up when my kayak idea turned out to be laughably inadequate. I might have given up when our first real boat sunk and we found ourselves shipwrecked.

Never mind the boats—I might have given up on Mozambique in general many times before that. I might have given up when people shot at me or when gangs were chasing me. I might have given up when we were in deep psychological distress after friends of ours in the Congo were dismembered in a church with machetes. I might have given up when I was reported in the newspapers as a drug dealer because of mistaken results at a lab, where they were testing some vitamins that were donated to us. I might have given up on the fifth, sixth, or seventh occasion when crowds began to stone me for preaching about Jesus.

Most especially I might have given up when my husband, Rolland, got cerebral malaria and suffered a series of micro strokes that almost killed him. Though he was eventually healed, for two years he lost his short-term memory and was totally unable to function in ministry or administration.

The only reason I did not give up at any of these times was because I know the One who placed His promises within me. When you know Him intimately, you never give up, because He is worthy!

You have to wait a long time for some promises. I was sixteen when the Lord told me I had a destiny in Africa, Asia, and England. It took me more than twenty years before I reached Mozambique and began to step into that piece of my calling.

Truthfully I am being overshadowed more now than I have ever been before. At times it is still very uncomfortable. There are days when I feel terribly stretched as God's promises grow within me, but even those days are a joy because I long to birth what God has given me.

Continue to carry your promises faithfully. Nurture them as they grow. It does not matter how old you are. It is never too late. The Lord wants to take you beyond who you are and what you can do. God is the One who can take a barren woman in her old age and make her fruitful for the first time, just as the angel told Mary:

> Even Elizabeth your relative is going to have a child in her old age, and she who was said to be barren is in her sixth month. For nothing is impossible with God.
>
> —Luke 1:36–37

Two things will come from being overshadowed. The first is a particular promise from God that is naturally impossible to fulfill. The second is a general promise from God that *nothing* is impossible with Him.

Our God is the God of the impossible. He can take a barren ministry and breathe His Spirit into it. Even in your old age He can breathe over you and cause you to bear a ministry, a promise, or a revelation—a beautiful gift that will carry His glory to the ends of the earth. He can take the most barren and broken life—even the kind of life that has aborted its own promises many times over—and in it plant a glorious new promise, along with all the strength that is needed to carry it to full term.

Chapter 11

ENTER INTO HIS REST

> *Therefore, since the promise of entering his rest still stands, let us be careful that none of you be found to have fallen short of it. For we also have had the gospel preached to us, just as they did; but the message they heard was of no value to them, because those who heard did not combine it with faith. Now we who have believed enter that rest.*
>
> —HEBREWS 4:1–3

THERE IS A place of rest in the heart of God. In this place we learn to trust Him in the midst of chaos and difficulties. As we lean upon Him and hear His heartbeat, we discover its rhythm—when to run, when to rest, and when to release. As we contend to enter into the rest He has prepared for us, we ourselves become resting places where He can come and dwell in greater fullness.

We can enter into the storms of life and release love only when we have learned how to rest in God. Hebrews 4:1–3 tells us to be careful not to fall short of His rest. Also, we will not achieve rest through the merits of our works, so that no one should boast (Eph. 2:9). Rather, we need to rest in the promises of God. We will be safe in the King's arms. Indeed, we must learn to live there.

Many things in my life threaten to steal my rest. The staff of Iris Global has grown so large—to over a thousand people—that the Mozambican government recently mandated unions for us. Hired union organizers have begun to march into our bases and start rallies. The first time one took place, it happened right outside my office and nearly turned into a riot. During that time I felt God saying to me that He simply wanted me to rest and not worry about it.

I admit that I am not always very good at this, but God keeps challenging me to go deeper and trust in His control. He encourages me that if we will take time to rest in Him, He will do more with our lives than we could ever hope to achieve otherwise.

Sabbath Rest

> There remains, then, a Sabbath-rest for the people of God; for anyone who enters God's rest also rests from his own work, just as God did from his.
> —HEBREWS 4:9–10

A Sabbath rest is one day a week. When told that they absolutely must rest, many people become frantic. "We need to go!" they say. "We need to run!" Often I am this sort of person myself.

Yes, we do need to run—but we also need to rest. This is part of the rhythm of God's heart. God has given a Sabbath rest for the people of God. Anyone who enters this rest also rests from his or her own work just as God did. God worked six days, and He rested on the seventh.

Of course, we do not just lie on the floor resting seven days a week. We would be sore and tired from resting! At the same time if we never rest, then we will never run. We cannot make it through our marathon without times of refreshing.

No can be an anointed word. We cannot be saviors to all. We are servants, daughters, sons, and brides, but not saviors. There is only one Savior. We cannot have His job.

We are called and allowed to rest. God is able to keep His world going, and in the meantime it is very important we do not do more than He is asking.

Some of us think the principle of rest does not apply to us. I assure you—it really does! We have to rest, beloved of God. You are going to get more accomplished through resting than through striving. It is important to take a Sabbath.

I try to pray for three to five hours every day. I get up early. I pray and I worship, and then I pray some more. Once I thought that could count as my Sabbath somehow, but later I found out God did not agree. He also wants me to play.

It was amazing to discover that God likes to stop and play. He told me one time to fly all of our senior leaders from the various nations in which Iris Global operates to Pemba. We were to play and pray. I asked if we could strategize as well. He said no!

We gathered on the *Iris Compassion* and drifted out to sea. We played and prayed—and ate! It might sound worthless in the natural, but God loved it. Some of us are so driven that we need to be very deliberate about learning to play—but I believe that if we learn how to play with our leaders and our friends, we will work together a lot better in the days to come.

Resting in the Ride

Let us, therefore, make every effort to enter that rest, so that no one will fall by following their example of disobedience.

—HEBREWS 4:11

I am incredibly tenacious. I know how to put in eighteen-hour workdays for many days at a time. I pushed hard through ten years of university to complete a PhD in systematic theology. I understand what it means to labor diligently.

I share these parts of my background so that you will not be tempted to think rest comes easily for me. But despite my personality, I have come to understand that we are commissioned to make every effort to enter rest. This may sound strange, but I grasp what it means because of how much warfare and contending it requires for me to secure a day off. It is much harder than fighting the curses of witch doctors. I am constantly asked to do just one more meeting or one more conference. It is not a simple thing for me to say no, but I do it for the sake of obedience.

I was once coerced into leading a meeting on one of those few days I was supposed to have off. I was exhausted and agitated. Nonetheless, Jesus came to the meeting. I could feel His presence strongly. Suddenly I had a vision. I saw myself sitting on a white horse. I love horses, but I was afraid because this white horse was galloping extremely fast.

I knew this was a picture of my life. It was an image of rapid revival and growth, of all the things I had seen birthed. I remember feeling sure I was going to fall from the horse. But then I sensed His voice saying, "Lean, Heidi, lean!"

I leaned in low over the horse's mane, and there was Jesus behind me, holding me in His arms. As I leaned, I was completely swallowed up inside His heart. We rode as one.

My concern over losing my precious day off dissipated into incredible joy. God had set me up. He did this because He wanted to show Himself strong in the midst of my fatigue and limitation. Once again He taught me it is all about Him.

God wants to take you into a greater place of rest. He wants to bring you to the place where you can continue to ride the white horse even as you lean completely into Him, resting safe and calm in the midst of storms, revivals, and all manner of great works.

Rest, Run, Release

Therefore, since we have a great high priest who has gone through the heavens, Jesus the Son of God, let us hold firmly to the faith we profess. For we do not have a high priest who is unable to sympathize with our weaknesses, but we have one who has been tempted in every way, just as we are—yet was without sin. Let us then approach the throne

> of grace with confidence, so that we may receive
> mercy and find grace to help us in our time of need.
> —Hebrews 4:14–16

Are you ready to approach God's throne? Do you want to draw nearer than you have ever been before? Do you want to feel His heart beating inside your chest?

Let us approach the throne of grace as little children. God is not unjust. He will not forget your work. He will not lose sight of the love you have shown Him as you have served others. Hold on to your faith firmly.

He has commanded you to rest. This does not mean being lazy, but holding firmly to the hope you have. He does not ask us to relax day and night forever. He asks that we imitate Jesus and all those who, through faith, inherited what was promised.

We have seen incredible disasters in Mozambique. In one of the worst disasters three hundred fifty of our churches were destroyed by floodwaters. Hundreds of thousands of people lost their possessions, their homes, and their crops. Many died.

In that situation I was obviously not thinking about sleep, but even at times like these some rest is important. The only way I know how to rest in such a disaster is to lean in and listen to the heart of God. In the rhythm of God's heart there is resting, there is running, and there is releasing.

Run, rest, release.

When I found out about that particular flood, I was at a conference in Canada. One of my Mozambican sons called me on the phone. He was terribly distraught, crying that people were dying and starving. He said it was one of the worst tragedies he had ever seen—and he had seen a lot.

God had been telling me that year to learn how to rest. I had no idea how to rest with my son screaming on the other line about the thousands of people suffering in my nation. How could I rest while so many were desperate and dying? But I felt the Lord asking me to trust Him and rest in the boat without fear.

I still did not understand. How could I rest in the boat when it seemed the nation was sinking? The phone rang incessantly. I was scheduled to speak in Canada for several more days.

God reminded me of the rhythm of run, rest, and release. As I continued to pray and listen, I heard Him saying it was now time to release. At first I did not know what He wanted me to release in the face of such a major disaster. Then I heard the Lord telling me to release my sons and daughters.

I started to call our Mozambican sons. Almost all of them had been homeless when we found them. Some had been thieves and bandits, but now they were all grown up and strong in the Lord. We released large sums of money into their hands so they could go and feed the hungry in the refugee camps. We released the keys to our trucks. I hesitated at that point, afraid they might crash all those trucks because they were not very experienced drivers, but I felt the Lord assuring me He was entrusting these young men with the trucks and with provision for their people.

Those who had been homeless for many years were now racing out to build homes for flood victims. They were absolutely diligent with finances. (One of them made a minister who went with him write a $0.03 receipt for using a public restroom!) I was astonished at how responsibly they handled the crisis.

When we arrived back in Mozambique, we found they had indeed crashed some of the trucks. God encouraged us to give them keys to different trucks. I wondered if that was wise, but I think God used this experience to teach us how much He trusts all His children. Sometimes we *are* going to crash the trucks. Sometimes we aren't going to get it right. We make mistakes. Papa God is releasing us anyway. He means to give all of us keys.

Before long the president, the governor, and the news media had interviewed our team of young Mozambican men and women. Their fellow countrymen spread the news of the ways in which they had come together to bless the nation. It was especially wonderful for me, as a mama, to hide in the back and watch as they shined.

If we will learn the rhythm of God's heart, we will not be afraid to release sons and daughters before they themselves know how they will be able to finish the race. God Himself will ignite their passion. They are going to run far ahead, and we will catch up breathlessly.

We have to release so many details in our lives. At one conference a lady came up to me shaking her head and said, "How do you cook for all those children?"

That was hilarious. I am no cook at all. I could burn water. She literally thought I cooked for thousands of children every day. Of course we have a huge team of cooks.

There are hundreds and thousands of people doing good and important things for God. No one is supposed to try to do it all. If we do not get into the rhythm of God's heart, we can forget this. We become overwhelmed and get burned out. Being good releasers enables us to rest instead.

We have to release life, release the Holy Spirit, release anointing, release leadership, and release people into their many diverse destinies.

Run the race. Learn how to lean into Jesus. Let Him hold you close until you can hear the rhythm of His heartbeat. Then you will know when to rest, when to run, and when to release.

Become a Resting Place

We need to enter into the rest God has prepared for us. We also need to learn how to become a resting place for Him to dwell. We need to become a temple where God is always invited to come and pour His oil into our lives. Cars without oil, even if they have gas in them, will not function. They need a steady supply of clean, fresh oil in order to move properly. I could write thousands of pages about the need to take in the harvest or God's healing glory, but unless we have a continuous provision of heaven's oil, we will never complete God's full calling. The good news is that at all times, God is ready to pour it freely over all who desire it.

I was reminded of this truth while lying in the hospital during a season of life when I was very ill. It was 2005, and I had been confined to a hospital in South Africa for over a month with a severe MRSA infection, which is a particularly robust kind of staph infection. I was literally dying. I took it as a lengthy opportunity for constant prayer and worship. I tried to focus on staying filled with the oil of the Holy Spirit.

This was one of the rare times I did not have people lining up to speak with me. A few of the nurses came in for prayer, but that was all. I was glad to pray with them. I remember how they said they felt so much life in my room. I think it is interesting that even while I was dying, there was still palpable life in my room. God is so good that He fills us with the oil of the Holy Spirit even when our bodies fade. In truth, we are only ever alive when the oil of His glory-love is filling us up inside.

While I was stuck in the hospital, I also had a lot of time to read Scripture. The Lord spoke to me as I was meditating on the Book of Zechariah. He told me He still looks for resting places where He can dwell. I noticed that the name *Zechariah* actually means "the Lord remembers."

After one doctor came and said I could write my own tombstone, I began to remind God of all His words to me. I reminded Him of His promise that we would take in a million children. I might be ninety-nine years old by the time we have that many, but I will see it accomplished.

I believe God likes His children to remind Him of His promises. Of course, He remembers all His covenants, but when we are able to speak out in faith concerning them, it gladdens His heart.

I told God I was ready to die but that I did not want to die from a flesh-eating disease. I wanted to keep sharing the gospel and ministering until the day Jesus took me home. I called upon His promises to me and feasted on what He revealed through the witness of Zechariah.

Still confined to my bed, I asked Rolland to buy me a new pair of running shoes. Rolland didn't tell me that I was a silly woman for requesting sneakers instead of hospital slippers. He drove right out and went to two different malls to find me the perfect pair.

They sat by my bed for weeks. I looked at them every

day. I couldn't wait to run. As sick and tired as I was, I had hope because I believed God had a destiny for me.

In Zechariah's day the people were exhausted from building the temple. They were so tired that they had stopped partway. God called for them to return to Him. He asked them to finish His house because He wanted to have mercy on them (Zech. 1:3).

Many of us have been in revival and renewal. We have seen the mighty things of God. There was a time when we were filled to overflowing, but then we grew tired. Sometimes we break down and stop building the things God called us to build.

Through His prophet God is asking us to finish what we have started. God began a mighty work in each of us. He is inviting us to participate in His divine nature. It requires all of us—all our life and all our years.

God also spoke to me about houses during that time of my illness. He showed me that my house—my body—had prophetic significance. I had a flesh-consuming disease that was trying to destroy my body. It was eating away stubbornly at my life and skin. It poisoned my system. There are things in the church too that eat away the life of the community and cause it to become weak.

God wants to fully inhabit His house. He wants His people to finish that which He has given them to do. He wants them to be full of life and power as they finish the task.

I reminded the Lord that I loved Him and that I had given my life for ministry. I had served Him day and night for thirty years. I asked Him what the purpose was in my suffering. I had seen Him cure blindness, deafness, and many diseases. Why had I not been healed?

All kinds of people prayed for me. I am sure God was thrilled with their prayers. Some called to ask if I was feeling better. Others told me to get up in the name of Jesus. By faith I would get up off the bed and tell them I felt better. At the same time I wished they would hang up right away because I was going to fall over.

I was fighting the good fight, but I was desperate. I felt that God showed me there is a spiritual fight we are waging together; its outcome determines whether or not we stay full of the oil of the Spirit. Finishing our task involves warfare. Sometimes we must accept its trials. I told the Lord to have His will and to make me a resting place for the Holy Spirit.

As difficult as that time was, the Lord was also very kind to me. A white dove fluttered outside my window every morning. It would come back in the cool of the evening and sleep there next to my window. It blessed me deeply because I knew God was speaking. He was asking if I would allow myself to be a resting place for His Spirit.

Of course I wanted to be. But I was still in a fight.

In the hospital God dealt with me concerning rest. I felt Him saying I was paying back the days from all of those weeks in which I would not rest for even one day. I had grown sick because I thought that I needed to do something for Him when what He most wanted from me was rest. For a short time I argued, reminding Him of my busy conference schedule and all of the Saturday meetings I was obliged to attend. God told me to change the day or find another one.

Obviously I did not want to stay sick. As much as I wanted to be full of love and passion, I also wanted to finish the race and win. I was not done yet. I did not want to leave this life from a hospital bed.

Through Zechariah God speaks about building His house. You are His house. You are the place where the Holy Spirit dwells (1 Cor. 3:16; 6:19). God is rebuilding His house and His people. He is expanding our hearts to carry more of His love. He is stretching us so we can hold more oil.

On my thirty-second day in the hospital I saw a specialist who told me they could do nothing more for me. He suggested going to a university hospital, where I might be able to participate in a clinical trial of some new "compassion antibiotics." In South Africa they had no cure for me.

Twice before I had been hospitalized for this same infection, and both times I had checked myself out of the hospital in faith, believing God would heal me. Instead the infection got worse. This was my third hospitalization. Now I did not seem to have much time left.

Sometimes we step out in faith for God and it does not appear to work. Have you ever done that? Sometimes we get too nervous to try again. We give up. But God wants to take that fear out of you.

At the end of this third hospital visit I felt God saying I needed to go to Toronto. The staff told me this was a stupid plan. Canada was all the way across the world, and its facilities were no better than South Africa's. I checked out of the hospital anyway. I knew my destiny was to live and not die because of all the promises God had already given me.

I had my running shoes next to my bed for a reason.

Sometimes when God wants to heal you, He may ask you to get up, go somewhere, or do something. You may need to do more than sit there, hoping for someone to touch you. If you have arthritis, He might say, "Get up and dance." If you have depression, He might simply say, "Rejoice!" It need not make sense to anyone else.

I said to Rolland, "We need to get on a plane right now and go to Toronto because God told me to."

I was scheduled to speak at a church there. When I was ill in the hospital, I had to cancel my speaking engagements, but I had not felt led to cancel this one. They did not really expect me to come because they knew I was sick, though at the time they did not know how severe my illness really was.

I arrived in Toronto pale as a ghost and extremely weak. I would have fallen over if someone had touched me. I had my running shoes packed in my suitcase though.

When they saw me, the leaders there were scared. They did not want me to die at their conference. They had a doctor there who wanted to hook me up with an IV immediately. They assured me I did not have to speak. I told them I had come a long way and that I was most definitely going to preach that night.

They were extremely nervous, but they let me have my way. I asked their doctor to lay his hands on me and pray instead of putting in an IV. Then, slowly, I managed to make my way up to the stage. God told me that I was to release the word from Zechariah.

I made it to the pulpit, holding on to it for dear life so I would not fall down. I began by quoting Zechariah 2:5:

"I myself will be a wall of fire around it," declares the LORD, "and I will be its glory within."

As I read the verse, all at once the glory of the Lord hit me. It felt like electricity going up and down my body. A torrent of God's fire went from my head to my toes three times. I was totally, completely, instantly healed. All the weakness and pain left my body. The sores completely closed up. Thirty-two days of the most intensive antibiotic regimen known to man had not worked, but in one moment with King Jesus all was well.

I was transformed right there in front of those people. They did not know the full significance of what had happened, but I knew and God knew.

The next day I put on my running shoes and jogged! It was truly miraculous.

Fire Around and Glory Within

God has promised to be a fire around us and the glory within us. He will protect and inhabit His people. We want God to be a wall of fire around us. We want His glory to fill up every corner of our beings. He wants a place where His glory can dwell. He is looking for resting places, houses, and living temples yielded completely to Him so He can come and inhabit them.

> "Shout and be glad, O Daughter of Zion. For I am coming, and I will live among you," declares the LORD.
> —ZECHARIAH 2:10

The Lord Almighty will live among us. He will dwell inside us. He fights for us because He loves His children. We must become familiar with the rhythm of His heartbeat. We must know when to run, when to rest, and when to release. That is how we will carry the dreams He gives us. There is something about cultivating our hearts to bring so much pleasure to the heart of the Father that causes the Holy Spirit to literally rest inside us.

He wants to know if there is someone who will never turn his thoughts to another, someone so full of love that He can rest inside him. You will not scare Him away. He loves to dwell in those who love Him. He loves to rest inside those who must have more of Him, who do not care what it takes, who are desperate for Him. The Lord looks across the earth for sons and daughters willing to be fully possessed. The Lord looks for a resting place.

Will it be you?

Chapter 12

EMBRACE *the* JOY
SET BEFORE YOU

*Therefore, since we are surrounded by such a great cloud
of witnesses, let us throw off everything that hinders
and the sin that so easily entangles, and let us run with
perseverance the race marked out for us. Let us fix our
eyes on Jesus, the author and perfecter of our faith, who
for the joy set before him endured the cross, scorning its
shame, and sat down at the right hand of the throne of
God. Consider him who endured such opposition from sinful
men, so that you will not grow weary and lose heart.*

—HEBREWS 12:1–3

W E HAVE A mighty calling to carry God's heart and to reveal His glorious love to the world. None of us can fully imagine or expect what the Lord has for us or what the journey to its fulfillment will look like. I don't think Mary was expecting to carry a child before she was married or to give birth to the Son of God. She could never have anticipated the magnitude of the call or the price she would have to pay.

I don't think any great thing we are called to do comes solely through us. Rather, the precious fruit of eternal significance comes when God's heart is manifested in and through us. As we walk obediently in the paths He sets for us, He reveals more details about what we've been created to do and how we are to do it. I believe the Lord, in His kindness, reveals our destiny to us in stages. He shows us His dream and His desire for the world.

We are paintbrushes in the hands of the Master. We cannot paint, but He can. I always say to God that if He can use a donkey, He can use me. He could use a rock if He wanted to. If we understand the cross, we know our lives are not our own; they belong to Him. We have been bought with a price. With that in mind, what then will we live for?

Our Lives Are Not Our Own

One day I was at a church conference in the Middle East when I found myself listening to a speaker who didn't know I was present. Evidently he had no idea I was scheduled to speak right after him. Since I was preparing to minister, I was surprised and dismayed when he began talking negatively about my life and ministry.

I wanted to hide. I wanted to run away and never speak there again. But first I prayed, and I felt the Holy Spirit reminding me that my life is not my own. I believed God had asked me to share in this place, so I obeyed. When I walked out on that stage, it felt like I was dying again.

Mercifully the Lord came and touched people with power. I became very aware, yet again, that my life is not my own.

If we are wise, we will make the choice to say yes to God many times each day. We say yes to taking the time to worship, to having a positive attitude, to releasing people, to stopping for people when we might be in a hurry, to trusting God for a seemingly impossible financial situation. Our yes is a daily choice. There is a daily sacrifice and a daily joy as we participate in God's dreams for this world. As we do this, we participate with Jesus in the sacrifices He too made for the joy that was set before Him. What an awesome privilege!

Working Together Brings in the Harvest

God wants to work through each of us using the personalities and giftings unique to us. Paintbrushes are all unique unless they are mass-produced, and then they are not very valuable. Brushes are all distinct and used for different things. God expresses His love through each of us in a unique way. After all, original works of art are far more valuable than copies. Even though we are only little paintbrushes or little pots, we are made individually, and no one else is like us. The Holy Spirit flows through each vessel, revealing God's dream for the world and our own place within it. What a glorious plan!

Even so, we cannot do the work of God all on our own. We need the hands and feet and hearts and minds of other people, all working together to bring God's great kingdom to fruition on the earth. We need each other.

I began to see this in even greater measure one day when I was praying with friends in Mozambique. During our time of prayer I saw a vision of a huge fishing net being let down from heaven. When I saw the net, I was thrilled because I thought it was a net for Iris Global, representing all the great work we would do and the growth we would see.

I felt as if the Lord chuckled and showed me that Iris Global was just a little piece of that vast net. He showed me some of the other pieces. I saw the Assemblies of God, the International House of Prayer, Bethel Church, the Toronto church, the Baptists, Youth With A Mission, the Nazarenes, Operation Blessing, World Vision, and many other movements across the earth. They were each serving and loving Him. I felt the Lord say that only when we work together will we bring in the harvest.

Part of my destiny is to see one million children brought home and cared for within my lifetime. I have come to realize the vision I saw of the fishing net has a lot to do with this destiny.

God has allowed me to pour my life into many people. I have had the privilege of imparting His heart for children and the poor around the world. When God ignites people's hearts in this way, they begin to rescue children. They feed them, house them, and educate them. The ones they care for are part of my vision for a million children. Ministers who have spent time at Iris and then left to begin their own organizations are also a part of it. The vision is not only for Rolland and me; it belongs to many faithful men and women around the world. It is a legacy for our children and our children's children.

Rolland and I believe we are called to cheer on the next generation of laid-down lovers. As they run into the darkness to love the broken and bring the lost children home, we want our ceiling to be their floor.

There is a price to raising up the next generation, but when we see them thrive, that cost seems like nothing. When a mother goes into labor, there is excruciating pain, pushing, and transition. There is incredible stretching. Blood vessels burst.

When I held my first baby, Elisha, and looked into his eyes, I completely forgot about the pain of childbirth. When we were ready to have another child, there was not a single moment when the prospect of pain made me think I could not do it again. When the time came, I held my daughter, Crystalyn, in my arms and felt the same awesome love. The joy of bearing a child is greater than the cost of suffering.

It is the same with spiritual things. When you see your sons and daughters raised up and saying yes to the destiny God extends to them, you feel blessed and privileged that you were able to pay a price to help them.

After sharing the gospel together for more than thirty-seven years, Rolland and I still minister together. We fall more in love with Jesus every day. If we had another thousand lifetimes, we would give them all away for love's sake. Every breath, every moment, everything we have—we would give it all!

As we have been getting older, we have been thinking a lot about legacy. Recently the Lord has put it on our hearts that we must seek to grow and support not only Iris Global but also a far wider move of God that encompasses hundreds and thousands of men, women, and children who are venturing fearlessly into the darkness of the earth for the sake of the gospel.

Here are some of the testimonies of our friends and spiritual children who have spoken a wholehearted yes to following the Lamb, no matter where He leads.

Cassandra Basnett: Releasing Love in War Zones and Brothels

I was in Mozambique as an unsuspecting eighteen-year-old. I had graduated from high school two months ahead of my classmates to attend Iris Global's first-ever missions school. I was so hungry for more of Papa that after feasting all day in classes, I would often take advantage of the nights and steal away for extra moments with my Jesus.

One evening when I was all alone, just lost in worship, the scenery transformed, and I was taken into a vision—to a war zone. My eyes opened up, and suddenly I was no longer in the comforts of student housing but in a pit with several dozen people. The air was thick with a weighty fear and a stench too foul to recognize. My mouth tasted of fresh blood that I assumed had something to do with the hard blow I felt come to my head. Looking around at the terrified faces surrounding me, I quickly learned what the panic was about. We were being buried alive! It was horrific. A group of soldiers was laughing and gawking. Killing us for sport was a game to them.

I cried out to God, "Where am I, and how on earth did I get here?"

Instantly the scene shifted. It was not any better. Suddenly I was a soldier. Looking down, I wore a broken pair of flip-flops and tattered army pants. "Oh, Jesus—this is worse!" I cried.

Another rebel punched my arm and nodded in approval

of my position. Crying out again, desperate for my Savior, I could not imagine what I would do if the vision carried on.

And then I saw Him—the very embodiment of peace and love. He entered the mob with such grace and humility. As I watched Him, He reached down and grasped one of my rebel comrades. Taking his hand, He pulled him close—so close. The young warlord was taken to the lap of Jesus. I have never seen such love in all my life. The gaze of His eyes was tangible, and I felt the core of who I was being transformed by simply watching their interaction.

The murderer, terrorist, and rapist met his Papa for the first time. Without condemnation he was taken in as His son, and they just held each other. It was a holy moment that left me absolutely speechless.

And then, shifting His glance for the first time, my Papa looked my way, and I sensed Him saying, "I hate what they do, but I love who they are—who I have made them to be."

Every bit of my previous "justice theology" was thrown out the window, and a whole new understanding of Papa's love flooded over me.

Here I was, the most unlikely of candidates: a young single girl without any fancy degrees, with no money, no terrific strategies, and terrified of public speaking. But my inadequacies seemed to be drowned out by the heartbeat of my Papa, crying out for a generation of pimps and lost warlords that He longed to father.

It was in that moment, while being completely lost in His love, without even a full understanding of what was going on and with every fiber of my being, that I cried out, "I will go! Send me to the rebel-held territories and hourly rate hotels! I will go to find Your favorites—to see You reunited."

And so He did.

From Mozambique Papa began to take me all over the world, wrecking me with even more of a passion to see restoration come to war zones and brothels, the pimps and the prostitutes, the warlords and the rape victims. Nothing seemed impossible in the arms of such a perfect Papa! Southern Sudan, Northern Uganda, the Democratic Republic of the Congo, Thailand—it was a journey of leaning on His voice for my every step, being wooed by my God in some of the most traumatic back alleys and hells of the earth.

As the dust settled and my time touring some of the darkest places shifted, I was left with homes in both the Congo's "UN classified" red zone as well as in a village that is built on sex work along the coast of Kenya—my starting grounds.

Now what? While still young and with nothing more than a set fixation on the flecks in His eyes, it has been "sink or swim." I quickly learned that it is in those secret places and longings of His heart that transformation comes. He is not looking for great personal qualifications or accomplishments based on merit; all He is looking for is your yes—that you would get so lost in His gaze that not even a rebel army could shake your confidence in who you are as His child.

Though my heart was burning for the soldiers and the sex-traffickers, my blonde ponytail seemed more of a hindrance than a door opener into the pits. It was then again that I saw that if any change would come, it would have to be 100 percent heaven's intervention. It kept me low and completely dependent, something that still resounded in my ears from my early days in Mozambique.

And He never let me down. Unlikely doors would open by grace to show love to a murderer or a sex offender and share Papa's heart. And time after time heaven would come, and lives were never the same, both theirs and mine.

Now, still without much understanding as to the "how," we have seen schools erected in conflict zones, businesses started, child soldiers rescued, and child prostitutes housed. The presence of God continues to expand as we go low and say yes, seeing impossibilities yield as we simply get lost in our perfect Papa's gaze.

Rabia Rene Emilio Ojomodave: From Orphan to Daughter and Mother

The old memories of when I lived in Centro Educacional de Chihango in 1995 are still so clear in my mind. I was an orphan, without a father or mother. My soul was often overwhelmed with feelings of abandonment and lack of love and care. I had absolutely nobody to share my feelings with.

That year the Lord sent His servant Mama Aida (Heidi) to Chihango. She introduced me to Jesus, the wonderful Savior of my soul, whom I have accepted as my Lord and to whom I have given my life.

My life completely changed. I was baptized and no longer felt abandoned because I had someone to share my pain with and to dry up my tears. Jesus became the source of my life.

Not long after that some difficult trials came our way. We were all expelled from the Chihango children's center by the government. Mama Aida and sixty of us children had to leave. We had nowhere to go, so she took us to her little office house. We went through many difficulties because she did not have enough money to feed all of us.

It was there that I saw a miracle for the first time in my life. The day this happened, we were all very hungry and had nothing to eat. All of a sudden a lady phoned Mama Aida and said she would prepare lunch and bring it to her family. But Mama Aida did not tell her that besides her immediate family, she had all sixty of us staying with her.

This lady prepared enough food just for Mama Aida and her family and brought it in little pots. When she arrived, Mama Aida called all of us together. Her friend became upset and asked Mama Aida why she did not tell her there were sixty extra children staying with her. Mama Aida responded that it was not a problem and that they were just going to pray.

After we prayed, we started serving the food. Then I saw with my own eyes that the Lord was multiplying it! The more we served, the more food we had. The food in the little pots never ran out. All of us ate, and we even had food left over.

Throughout the years I have been through many trials. But in all the difficulties I went through, I never felt like Jesus abandoned me. He was, He is, and He will always be with me. I have learned that the roots of the believer grow deeper when we go through trials.

One of the greatest difficulties I have been through in my life was with my husband. He went through a phase when he started to take drugs and drink alcohol. He smoked and slept with prostitutes. Sometimes he would come home late at night while I was sleeping, bring other women into our own bedroom, and have sex with them right there. I persevered in much prayer, and I had faith that we would overcome these problems. And God did intervene in our lives. One of the women my husband slept with became pregnant with his baby. She did not want the baby, so I decided to take him home to live with our family and to bring him up as my own son. My husband got completely transformed. Today, besides our own children, we are also taking care of some other young men, who like me at Chihango have had no one else to take care of them.

> Commit your way to the LORD; trust in him and he will do this: He will make your righteous reward shine like the dawn, the justice of your cause like the noonday sun.
>
> —PSALM 37:5–6

I thank the Lord for everything that has happened in my life. I believe that just as it says in the Word of God, those who believe in Jesus will never be disappointed.

Jennifer Mozley: Missions in Africa and China

My background is not one of a long line of ministers. I did not know much about mission life—or Christianity, for that matter—until I met Jesus in a holy and powerful way when I was twenty-nine years old. As I began to walk in this new life in Jesus, my heart always cried out, "I will go anywhere You want me to go, but if You are not with me, I don't want to go!"

The first time I heard the Holy Spirit call me to China was at the Iris base in Maputo around Christmastime in

2002. I was walking in the kitchen by myself when I heard the Holy Spirit clearly say, "China."

I did not know what this meant at the time at all. Why would I be in Africa and hear China? The next year my new husband and I returned to the Maputo base, and I heard Holy Spirit say again, "China." How wild is that? A nation I did not know burned in my heart more deeply than any other! I had never been to China, nor did I know anything about it.

My husband and I began to pray about quitting our jobs and going into full-time ministry. We loved what we were experiencing in Africa every Christmas as we visited the Iris base. We were feeling God's leading to Pemba, Mozambique, to serve with Iris Global.

Two years before we moved to Africa and enrolled in the Harvest School of Missions, I went alone to a prayer meeting while my husband, Mark, was out of town. The leader of the prayer meeting, a good friend of ours, started prophesying over me that he heard God say Mark and I would go to China and do a lot of great things there. Then, about thirty minutes later, a young gentleman came to the prayer meeting not knowing anything that had been prayed over me. He interrupted the prayer time and said, "Ma'am, I don't know who you are or what this means, but I keep seeing a map of China over you." He told me the name of the city, and then he proceeded to tell me some very specific things about my life that only God could have known.

This really got my attention! He continued to prophesy about what God wanted to do through us in China and how we would see the Lord move in a mighty way among people groups in the country. I was doubled over on the floor as he prophesied these things. The power of the Lord was on me in a holy way, and I could not ignore what was being said. So I started to journey with the Holy Spirit in prayer as He continued to speak to my heart about China over the next two years.

After that prayer meeting, the next day I went to work and climbed up on my desk to look at the huge world map hanging above my workstation. I asked God to show me where this particular city was. God was faithful to answer that prayer quickly and highlighted to me that place in China. It was amazing!

About two years later the Lord spoke to us to first go to Africa and serve with Iris (if they would have us!). Mark also received several confirmations from the Lord about Africa. At first I was fearful about going, until I went to a conference in London that year where Rolland Baker was speaking. At the conference God impacted me deeply with confirmation that Africa was the place to go. I was so undone after Rolland prayed for me. He spoke things to my heart that released me from all fear. I surrendered that night to the Lord's heart for us to travel to Africa.

Mark and I went through the 2007 summer missions school and stayed on after the school had ended. We had a curriculum of books to read during our time in this school. One of the books was about Rolland's grandparents, who had a group of young, poor orphan boys who came under such a powerful move of the Holy Spirit. They saw visions of heaven and hell and experienced waves of repentance for their sins—all without previous Bible knowledge and teaching.

But what got my attention as I began to read the book was where this took place in China—it was the very city

God had spoken to me about two years earlier! Wow! I found out it was also the birthplace of the founder of the ministry that I was going to serve. I was blown away. During our time in school the Lord connected us with missionaries who were already serving in that city. They were visiting Pemba during this time, which was unusual, as they did not come there very often.

We served in Pemba for over two years before we heard anything else from the Lord about serving Him in China. But in the summer of 2009 He began to move on both of our hearts that it was time to transition to our new home in Asia. We moved there in 2010 and are beginning to see waves of revival spring up. We are ready to pick up the mantle H. A. Baker left in that city and take it on to new heights in the Spirit!

Mark Mozley: Encountering the Presence of God

Growing up within the Western church, I always had a tension with what the Bible actually said versus how my life reflected it. In reality they were many miles apart. It was as if the Bible was a book of make-believe. I was a tongue-speaking charismatic who could recite the verses and decree the promises, but I knew nothing of true intimacy with Jesus, the true power of the Holy Spirit, or the true love of the Father.

Then in July 2002 Heidi Baker came to our church. For the next three days my life was turned completely upside down. The presence of God strongly descended upon the meeting as she shared. I felt Jesus encounter me from the first few words that came out of her mouth. I do not think it was because she said anything particularly profound, but the stories she told of her life among the poor in Mozambique burned like fire in my heart. God was in those stories, in her message, and in her life. His presence was tangible. All at once everything changed. Could it be that the Bible was real after all? Could all the stories and promises from Jesus in this Book actually be experienced now?

I soon concluded that the reality of living a true kingdom life was not only possible but was also apparently happening in the life of Heidi, her husband, Rolland, and the children she worked with in Mozambique. I melted and wept after the message at the altar for hours and hours. I was so happy and also so sad that my life up until then had been filled with such "straw" and hypocrisy. I was crying on my face, unable to move because I was in the presence of the uncreated One. For the first time in my life I was truly encountering God—and like Isaiah, as a man of unclean everything, I could not stand up. The holy One was there, and nothing else mattered. A thousand sermons, a hundred books, or a dozen conferences could not have replaced the impact of this encounter. I was undone, and for the first time in my life He was truly all that mattered.

After the conference I made plans with my friend Jennifer to go and visit the Bakers in Mozambique. Six months later we went and encountered God over and over in the dirt. We loved on the children, witnessed miracles in the outlying villages, and just sat with people who were finishing the Book of Acts.

We returned home, and everything about my life and ministry changed. These significant encounters had to lead to change. This new wine demanded new wineskins. Church life changed. The Sunday events no longer satisfied me. We took to the streets and preached and prayed for the sick. We did all we could to prove that the Book was real and that an encounter with Jesus was possible. My friend Jennifer and I got married and returned to Africa two times in the next three years. Each trip found us falling more in love with Jesus and more unable to conduct our lives as usual back at home. We had the awesome privilege of moving to Mozambique to work with Iris Global in 2007. Then in 2010 we felt Father's call to move east and work with Iris Global in Asia, where we are presently.

Our ministry theme is still the same. Once you encounter Jesus, everything changes. Our job is simple—to set people up for that encounter and to prepare the way for the Lord, as John the Baptist modeled so well. And once they meet this Jesus, who has been longing to meet them all their lives, we walk with them through the process of continuing to encounter God and empowering others to do the same. The kingdom of God comes, and discipleship happens. May we never deviate from this one thing—that our fruit flows from intimacy and that this intimacy flows from encountering the Father's love.

Lyle Philips: Modern-Day Abolitionist

Face-to-face with slavery

My first encounter with child slaves shook me to the core. I did not know how to process it. Here I was, standing over the edge of a massive cliff in India, looking below at hundreds of small children who were working frantically to hoist large pieces of slate rock from a quarry.

These children were filthy, half-naked, malnourished, and abused. As I began to wander down into this rock quarry with a few friends, I was met by a man who introduced himself as the boss. He obviously did not like the idea of us going any further. We wanted to obey the man's instructions but were able to convince him we wanted to do nothing more than to visit some of the children. Although we were not permitted to move on, he did allow a few of the children to approach us from the quarry.

I met a little boy and a little girl. The girl looked to be about twelve, but she had no idea of her age. The boy said he was nine. As I looked into this little girl's eyes, I could see the abuse, the pain, and the desperation. I knew she needed help. She was forced to work in terrible conditions for more than ten hours a day, all just for one meal. She had three older sisters who had once worked alongside her, but they had all committed suicide. What made things worse was that each night she was being raped multiple times by older men working in the quarry and sold to friends of the boss.

Stop for the one

In 2008 I found myself sitting on the floor under a thatched roof in the sweltering heat of an African summer. I was listening to Mama Heidi Baker preach to more than one hundred ministers from around the world. I had never heard stories like hers. I had never seen a lifestyle like the one she modeled. I wanted it. I wanted to become a laid-down lover of Jesus! I wanted to love and serve the poor as she did.

It was there in Mozambique, Africa, that I learned about the humble heart of Father God. It was there that I was called to ministry. One day at the Iris Harvest School of Missions I heard Heidi say, "We are all called to the nations, but to which nation? What people group? Who will you lay down your life down for?" In that moment I began to press into God's specific plan for my life as a minister and to ask Him which nations were mine.

In the coming months God showed me India and several other nations. I had never been to India and did not know anything about it. I did not have any natural affections for the nation and did not even like Indian food!

After arriving home from Mozambique, I began preparing my heart in prayer for my visit to India. I prayed and fasted often. I read Indian news and watched Indian movies. Around that time CNN released a report stating there were an estimated 1.2 million child prostitutes in the nation of India.[*]

I knew the time to go would be soon, and I knew exactly what I wanted to do once I got there: rescue child prostitutes.

And there I was, face-to-face with a child prostitute in a rock quarry in India. Everything I had prepared myself for in prayer and at the Iris Harvest School of Missions was now front-row and center.

"We are going to get you out of here," I told the young girl, but she looked away in disbelief, without any hope.

"No, I promise," I told her through an Indian translator. We were stopping for her. No matter what the cost, no matter what the responsibility, this little girl was coming home with us to receive love and proper care.

We spent three days negotiating for her freedom. It ended up costing us everything we had in our bank

[*] CNN, "Official: More Than 1M Child Prostitutes in India," May 11, 2009, http://edition.cnn.com/2009/WORLD/asiapcf/05/11/india.prostitution.children/ (accessed August 27, 2013).

account to rescue her and the other little boy. We broke the bank for her.

The day I was leaving India was the day she was officially released. I had to leave early in the morning to catch my flight, so I was unable to escort her to her new home, our first Iris home for children in Andhra Pradesh, India. But I was able to talk to her on the phone. In tears, with the few English words she understood, she repeated "thank you" over and over again until I too was a thankful wreck for Jesus while boarding my flight back to the United States.

We are abolitionists!

This little girl and little boy were the first child slaves and prostitutes I had ever met—the first child slaves and prostitutes rescued by Iris Andhra Pradesh. And that was just three years ago. Today we feel like bystanders as God continually shows up and shows off in these rock quarries.

The bosses are being saved too. Jesus is encountering them in dreams and visions. Children are being released—more than just one or two at a time for high prices. To date we have seen more than four hundred children released and rescued from these rock quarries. They are received into one of our eight homes for children, positioned throughout the state of Andhra Pradesh. In total, Iris Andhra Pradesh is taking care of sixteen hundred children at the time of this book's writing.

What began as a prayer in Pemba, Mozambique, has now become a living work amongst some of the poorest, most desperate people in the world. I live in India throughout some of the year and pastor an Iris church in Nashville, Tennessee, during the rest.

If I have learned anything by becoming part of the Iris

family, it is this: revival truly does begin with the poor! Heidi and Rolland are my spiritual parents, and it is my great honor to lay down my life alongside them for Jesus. The cost is great, but the reward is His, and He is worthy!

Nick and Marlene Boyd: Our Yes for His Glory

When we finally gave God our yes and moved halfway around the world to Tete, Mozambique, to rescue orphaned boys living on the streets, we knew our yes would not always be easy. We moved to Mozambique one month after we got married. We had a pretty good idea that our new adventure to change the world would have its challenges. Little did we know how big those challenges would be.

At 2:00 a.m. on February 21, 2013, our lives were forever changed. Two men showed up at our house, attacked our guard, tied him up, and dropped him in the bush across the road. They broke the locks off our back gate, pried open our back door, and entered our home.

The two men proceeded to the front of our house and entered the bedroom where Brooke, our intern, was sleeping. They tied up her hands, and one of the men tried to rape her. They asked her if anyone else was in the house and said that if she screamed they would kill her. She told them we were in the house, so they made her take them to our bedroom. They told her to only say our names so we would open the door. They said if she tried anything else, they would take her life.

She called out to Marlene and I (Nick) with a cry.

Marlene jumped up, squeezed my arm, and said, "Babe, there's someone in our house!"

I jumped up with my heart pounding out of my chest and looked for something to grab to hit whoever was outside our bedroom door. I found a heavy object and opened the door, but before I could do anything, there was a machete to my throat and two men were pushing their way into our room. They threw us all down on the bed and told us there were eight more men outside with guns, so we should not try anything stupid.

As they began to tie us all up, Marlene told the men they didn't have to steal. She told them Jesus loved them and died on a cross for them, that He has a purpose for their lives. She told them Jesus could be their provider the same way He had provided for us.

The men told her to shut up. They did not want to hear anything about our God. Then one of them grabbed my wife and dragged her to another bedroom. My heart sank. I knew I had to get my hands untied so I could try to overtake the guy holding us with a machete and rescue my wife.

As I tried to get them untied, I heard my wife scream. I lunged for the attacker in front of me. He slammed me back on the bed with the machete to my throat, threatening to take my life if I moved again. I have never felt so helpless in my life. All I could think was, "What is this man doing to my wife?"

I pleaded Jesus's blood over her to protect her. After only a few minutes the man dragged her back into our room and threw her on the bed. He stuffed a whole T-shirt in her mouth and tied it so she could not spit it out. Marlene could not breathe and began to have a panic attack. She looked as if she was about to die as she gasped for air. I pleaded for the attacker to just take my life and spare my wife. He finally loosened the T-shirt so she could breathe again.

They proceeded to tear our house apart, demanding money and anything else valuable. They took almost everything we had, loaded it into our luggage bags, and went out the back door.

Marlene's revelation of unconditional love during the attack

About one month prior to the attack Jesus began preparing me (Marlene) for what was to come. He asked me to dedicate all of my mornings to soaking, reading the Word, and spending time with Him. I truly believe that if I had not had this preparation time, I would have been full of rage, anger, and hatred toward these men instead of having compassion, knowing they did not know our Savior.

I never fully understood unconditional love until the night we were attacked. While I was tied up in a room separate from my husband and being sexually abused, the only thing I could do was pray for Jesus to have mercy on my attacker. That prayer ran through my mind over and over.

Jesus showed me a glimpse of what unconditional love looks like. Now I realize how Jesus could love me and die for me before I even loved Him or knew Him. For that I will be forever thankful.

More revelation a week after the attack

While recovering in Pemba after reading hundreds of messages from people who could not understand why we were not packing up our bags and going back to the United States, I (Marlene) began to ask Jesus why we did not feel the way the world said we should. Most people said we should hate these men and want to get revenge on them. I wondered if something was wrong with us.

I sensed that Jesus's response was, "What if I allowed these men to come and do what they did because I knew that you would love them and share My name with them? What if I knew that you might be the only one to speak to them about Me? What if that was their only chance to hear that I died for them and that I have a future and purpose for their lives?"

He asked me twice and waited for me to answer. My answer was that it was worth it all then. Our heart, our passion, and our mission are to share the gospel and the love of Jesus with everyone He places in our path. I am humbled that in the hardest situation Jesus chose me to be His voice and share His unconditional love.

Our love for God and for our boys is what keeps us going daily. Every day is not easy, but we rest in knowing Jesus already paid the price on the cross. He has called us to be a light in dark places, to love the unlovable, and to change the world one person at a time.

Mary-Ann: Beauty in Prisons and War Zones

At nineteen, with passport in hand, I was ready to leave England to start on a journey of discovery in encountering God. With no other ambitions in life I determined to spend my life traveling the world to search out someone who could show me the way. Seeing so much suffering in the world led me to believe that a revolution was needed, but I did not know what that was. My heart burned with questions no one could answer. Unexpectedly, before I even left my bedroom, the Holy Spirit visited me powerfully, and I knew for the first time that Jesus was very real and in pursuit of my heart.

I became convinced that when Jesus spilled His precious and royal blood onto the dirt of the earth, it was the single most profound and final statement of God's outrageous love for humanity. The light of this powerful love was far greater than any darkness that could ever exist. There should be no place in the world too dreadful, fearful, or evil for us to carry it.

To see God's glory as Moses had seen it became my daily prayer. I also begged with all of my heart to be sent to the places no one else wanted to go and that others ran away from. I often found myself crying out for my brothers and sisters in Christ who were going through extreme suffering for their faith.

I felt the Lord showed me that He would answer the cry of my heart and that I would see His glory, but that it would be in unexpected places: in the eyes of the poor and among the most despised ones of the earth, including the terrorist, prisoner, and sex offender. I felt Him say He would send me to places where the greatest suffering in the world existed and that in those places I would see His beauty and reveal the love of the cross.

Revolution of love

Some years later, when I heard Heidi Baker speak at a conference, everything in my spirit resonated with what she was saying and with how tangibly she carried the love of Christ. She embodied the very revolution that I had become convinced the world needed. It was a revolution of love!

Not long after I found myself in the prisons and jails of

the third world nation of Mozambique, serving with Iris Global. When I looked at the malnourished and ragged prisoners as I visited them, I was struck by how beautiful they were; I could see the image of God in them so clearly. I told these men the good news, that they were not forgotten, that their names had been engraved on the palm of God's hand. The King was in pursuit of their precious hearts.

Community of love

The Lord began to encounter the men powerfully through dreams and visions. Extraordinary miracles became usual. Sight and hearing were restored, symptoms of malnourishment disappeared, and old injuries were healed. Tormenting nightmares stopped, and the pain of loneliness and shame was washed away.

I loved visiting the special cell for victims of AIDS, tuberculosis, and the most severe diseases to tell them how precious and lovely they were. They were shocked, not only by the words they heard but also that a white woman from a prosperous nation would choose to leave behind family and friends to come and visit them in their desperately lowly state. The broken felt loved, often cripples walked, and transformation began to take place among this community of criminals, which was fast becoming a community of love.

Many brothers received creative gifts supernaturally. Some suddenly began speaking English and became translators. Others became artists and started to draw dreams the Lord gave them. Yet others received musical abilities they previously had not had. Jesus died that we would live life in all its fullness (John 10:10). He is not a God of half-measures!

"How can I be saved?"

The presence of God became very tangible. At times, as I walked down the corridor, prisoners would stop me and call out to me in desperation, asking me to pray for them. They asked me how they could change. They asked me how to be saved and follow Jesus. These were truly holy and unforgettable moments.

One day during a meeting a brother testified that Jesus had come to him in a dream and told him to come to our meeting to get saved. This was not an uncommon occurrence.

The demand for Bibles was often beyond what we could meet. The brothers insisted on having a Bible school in their prison because they were desperate to learn more about the Word of God.

As visitors from other nations came, they would often become aware of the presence of God as soon as their feet stepped onto the prison grounds. Visitors come to Mozambique to encounter God, but they do not expect that it will happen in the prisons. Many weep as they experience God's power among the least of these.

> I was in prison and you came to visit me.
> —MATTHEW 25:36

The lasting fruit of changed lives and transformed hearts even affected the police and prison guards. As the reputation of God's acts spread, doors to other prisons and jails opened.

We laid hands on those who were leaving and

commissioned them as apostles, evangelists, and sons of God. Those who were transferred to other facilities took the fire and love of God with them. Some of those who went back to their own homes and provinces also started prison ministries. Many were reconciled with estranged family members and friends. Households came to Jesus, and communities were greatly affected by the transformed lives they saw.

Hope in the midst of famine and war

After several years of learning from my brothers in the prisons and jails of Mozambique, the Lord led me into a closed nation in Africa that was in the grip of a horrific famine. The stories of mothers laying their babies by the side of the road to die as they desperately searched for food pierced my heart. This seemingly hopeless nation had been in constant war for more than two decades and was often referred to as the nation that God forgot. With no government in place, anarchy, terrorism, and lawlessness thrived. My heart broke for the people who were living in dread under the rule of warlords and extremists. As I asked Jesus to send me there, I saw a vision of my feet standing in the midst of the chaos declaring His love. I felt like I had a mandate from heaven to pray and declare hope and goodness over the land.

It was my imprisoned brothers who laid hands on me to commission me to go. It was these same ones who committed to pray for me while I was there.

Beauty in the eyes of the dying

The Lord wonderfully provided the money for my airfare on my way to the travel agent's office. The next day I found myself in what was commonly referred to as the most dangerous city in the world. It was a miracle to get into a nation where strict security arrangements were mandatory even before entering. The army had to release me from the airport into the care of an armed security convoy.

However, divine favor prevailed, and somehow there was access to government officials' offices. We also were given access to the desperately needy camps, where hundreds of thousands of internally displaced people gathered together in hopes of finding help. Some of them ate only once a week. This was the epicenter of reportedly the worst famine in recorded history.

The sight of starving babies and adults all around me trying to find shelter under bombed-out rubble was horrific beyond description. Nothing could have prepared me for what I saw. I was faced with suffering beyond anything I could have imagined in my whole life. A doctor told me that many still died even after they got their physical needs met due to hopelessness. These people had witnessed too much trauma to want to live. I learned the shocking truth that hopelessness can kill as much as a physical disease can.

As soon as I walked into the first camp, I saw a child lying on the ground, motionless with flies gathering around its mouth. The mother was helplessly looking on. I could not walk past without stopping. I felt compelled to somehow express compassion and comfort. As I held the fragile, skeletal frame of this dying infant in my arms and looked into her glazed and sunken eyes while the sound of bullets rang overhead, I saw God's indescribable beauty. My life was forever changed. Jesus branded my heart all over again for the most vulnerable, the helpless, and the dying. In that moment I felt my heart become intertwined with this war-ravaged nation.

Playgrounds in war zones

Since that time my heart has not stopped burning for this forgotten nation and its unreached people. Soon after my initial visit the Lord led me to start a charity focusing specifically on the restoration of places affected by extreme disaster and war. This was a great surprise and a great joy. However, it meant that once again I was faced with the cost of leaving everything behind in order to step into the next season of my destiny.

I keep going to this nation (which I now consider home) as often as I possibly can to continue the mandate of declaring God's hope and His unending goodness over the land. Since my first visit I can honestly say the suffering I have seen and experienced has been far greater than anything I could have imagined or even thought could exist in this world. It is simply beyond words.

However, I feel more compelled than ever to give my life fully to releasing love and hope in the most evil places of the world, regardless of what that might cost. I have a vision of playgrounds and parks being built in war zones as beacons of hope and of desperate people beginning to gather around laughter instead of grief and despair. I have a vision of children who have been made to carry guns or who have spent their lives locked up and chained as sex slaves playing freely and beginning to dream. This, to me, is a piece of what God's glory and beauty looks like.

Rolland and Heidi Baker are an exceptional example of those who search out and see God's beauty in the most broken places. Heidi's life of radical love and outrageous generosity provokes me whenever I am around her. She has given her life unreservedly and has paid a greater price than anyone will ever know so that a generation can be provoked to carry God's revolution of love into the darkness. It is a great honor and privilege to run this race of love shoulder to shoulder with one of my greatest heroes and best friends.

Chapter 13

SUPERNATURAL BIRTH

With God all things are possible.
—MATTHEW 19:26

I HAD A VISION several years after coming to Mozambique in which the Lord showed me how He was going to release a movement of supernatural love across the face of the earth. In this vision I was taken up to heaven and suspended above the earth. Around the earth, surrounding the entire globe, I saw thousands upon thousands of chariots of fire. They were carrying the glory of the Lord.

Inside each chariot sat two saints of God. They were totally transparent; there was nothing hidden in them. There was no darkness, nothing disguised, nothing covering them. They were transparent and full of glory, full of light.

There was only one spot of color inside each saint. It was a huge, immense heart that went shoulder to shoulder. It was a heart beating with love and passion. It was a huge red heart.

I looked up to heaven, and there was Jesus. He is so beautiful. His eyes of love were looking upon me, melting me, causing my heart to go bigger still.

I saw His heart, and it was beating. I saw it beating, and I heard it beating. I looked in the chariots at the saints of God, and each huge heart of love was beating in rhythm with the heartbeat of Jesus.

Each saint held a gleaming white-gold sword, and flames of fire were coming off them. It took two hands—two holy hands—to hold each sword.

Two white magnificent horses led each chariot. They were ready to run! They had veins on their necks and bits in their mouths. The reins were reaching straight up to heaven.

The Lord Jesus said to me, "Tell the church, 'Release control.' I will hold the reins to this revival. I will decide where the chariots run. Tell the church to release the reins to Me. Holy is the Lamb."

And then I saw the Lord's right hand straight above His head, and He cried, "Now!" As His right hand went down, the chariots of fire and glory began to run across the face of the earth.

As the chariots ran across the earth, glory fire fell upon the earth. Glory fire began to burn upon the earth, and the earth was ablaze.

But there were pockets on the earth that resisted the glory, the mercy, and even the love of Jesus. Those pockets upon the earth became hideous darkness like nothing I had ever seen. There were holes of hideous darkness like something I could never have imagined.

I looked at my Jesus, and He said, "The sword is both mercy and judgment. For those who will receive My love, there is great mercy, compassion, kindness, and glory, but for those who will reject My presence, My purpose, My love, there is great darkness and judgment."

I saw the gray that was upon the earth disappear. There was only darkness and light—and the light increased until the earth became ablaze with fire wherever the chariots ran. Where the transparent saints with huge hearts of love ran across the earth, there was great light, for the love of Jesus conquered the darkness through them.

The Lord asked me to ask the church who would ride in the chariots of glory—who would carry the huge heart of Jesus's love within them. Who would ride in the chariots of glory and not touch or steal the glory? Who would take the holy sword of the Lord in their hands? Who would release control to the Bridegroom King? Holy, holy is the Lamb!

The Time Is Now

The Lord also spoke to me through the birth of one of my grandbabies in Mozambique. One of my adopted sons, Jacinto, and his wife, Katie, were about to have their second child. I was very excited about this birth. I had also been present at the birth of their first son, Micah.

There was only one problem: Katie went into labor just before I was scheduled to fly out of the country on a speaking tour. I was in a meeting with Jacinto when we heard the labor had started. I nearly panicked when I checked my watch and saw that I had just one hour before I needed to board my plane.

Their first baby had taken thirty hours to be born. I

could not wait that long. And Katie certainly did not want another such lengthy labor either!

When I got to the house, Katie was only one centimeter dilated. I watched this beautiful spiritual daughter of mine screaming in pain, and at that moment I wanted nothing more than for it to stop. The doctor wanted her to try walking around a bit, so I held her hand and began to walk with her while praying in the Spirit.

Suddenly a strong prophetic urge came over me. The Lord stirred my heart, and I began to declare that she would go from one centimeter dilated to ten—*now*. Our startled doctor stared at me, but I went on declaring the word loudly. I believe that as I spoke the word over Katie, and other intercessors were also praying, an amazing miracle happened.

Suddenly Katie went into full labor. Her baby came supernaturally quickly. It had only been forty-five minutes since the strong contractions began when she gave birth to a beautiful baby boy. It might have been the easiest birth I have ever seen.

She named her boy Daniel Timothy.

I lifted up my grandchild to Jesus, and I dedicated him to Father God. Then I handed him to Jacinto and left for the airport and got on the plane just in time.

When we go through painful seasons and trials in our lives, we do not want our suffering to be prolonged. I believe Katie's child was released supernaturally quickly as a prophetic sign for the times. Many of you have been given prophetic words and promises that would seem to require long and difficult transitions before they could ever come to pass. You may have begun to feel that these promises are never going to come true because there is not enough time left for you to see them fulfilled. I believe this word is for you and that now is the time for God's promise to be supernaturally birthed in your life.

A few months later another spiritual daughter, Dominique, who was in Atlanta, was due to give birth to her first baby. She had heard the testimony of Daniel's supernatural birth and received it as a word personally for herself. She had decided that when she went into labor, she would text me so I could pray the *now* word for the birth of her child. However, she did not even have time to text me because everything happened so fast!

Dominique had been having some cramps during the day but did not think they were labor cramps. She kept working to help coordinate an Iris relief team that was going to the Philippines after the floods. (Dominique leads our Iris Philippines base.) Late that evening the cramps had not eased up, so Dominique and her husband, Aaron, decided to go to the hospital. At the hospital she was told that her cervix was closed and that it would be another two weeks, so she was sent home.

When Dominique got home, she said to Jesus that if this was the day her baby was supposed to be born, she accepted it, even though he would be born two weeks early. Moments after saying those words, her water broke. The pain increased exponentially, so she woke up Aaron. He called the midwife, even though they had not had the chance to make a birthing plan yet. As soon as she came, they all got in the car and headed to the hospital.

Fifteen minutes into the drive Dominique broke the silence and cried out from the backseat of the car that the baby was coming. The midwife told her not to push yet. In the middle of a contraction Dominique responded that she was not pushing, but the baby's head came out! The midwife looked over, shocked. Aaron was driving fast now! The midwife told him he would need to pull over so that Dominique could push. She did not even finish her sentence and the baby was completely out! The midwife caught the baby and sat back relieved. Dominique laughed over her baby boy. They told Aaron to keep driving. The baby was perfect. He was breathing and healthy. Aaron started crying, laughing, and shaking. He could no longer remember where the hospital was. It took them twenty more minutes to find the hospital. Dominique had had the baby within an hour of her water breaking!

A month earlier when a friend, Mary-Ann, prayed for Dominique, she had a vision of angels attending the birth as midwives, having so much fun. Little did Dominique and Aaron know what that really meant! Dominique felt that her son, Arie, being born in the car on the way to the hospital was a prophetic sign. Cars often represent ministry. This was clearly a sign of acceleration. The next day, at the dumpsite in the Philippines, a girl deaf in one ear since birth was completely healed. Dominique and Aaron felt this healing was directly connected to the acceleration they would see in the miraculous realm in their ministry.

Both of these births are a powerful prophetic sign for God's people. The transition has come, and it is time for the babies of God's promises to be born in our lives. It is time to bear the most precious of fruits. A natural birth is often long and painful, but God is ready and eager to perform miracles of supernatural swiftness on behalf of His children. On this very day He is even more eager than we are to see all of us coming together into the fullness of our destinies. He longs for us to grow up into the fullness of His Son—Jesus Christ.

It is time to go from one to ten *now!*

Accept Your Commission

As Rolland and I reflect back over the years, it is clear we never anticipated how high the cost of our calling would be. Likewise, I think Mary could not have known the extent of the pain she would have to go through—including watching her own Son crucified.

We also never anticipated the unceasing joy. We have witnessed incredibly abundant fruit, both in our lives and the lives of those walking alongside us in this beautiful movement that has flowered so far beyond our dreams.

We continually hear stories of people so touched by the Lord that they feel compelled to yield up their whole lives in return. Some come to work at one of Iris Global's bases located around the world. Others start their own projects and organizations. We rejoice in them all. It is our privilege to see so many saying yes to the joy and the cost of life in the secret place. More than anything we want to see a multiplication of His manifest love in the world.

Rolland and I recently hosted about two hundred of our national and international senior Iris leaders from around the world. These Global Team meetings were held on the very land where we are building a university to train Mozambican leaders to transform their nation. This property involves a nine-and-a-half-year journey. The Lord spoke to me to build a university while I was snorkeling one day. I was in total shock and sucked water into my throat! Later the Lord spoke to me about the time He healed me from severe dyslexia when I was sixteen years old and a baby Christian. My high school teachers told me I would never go to university and should simply pursue vocational training, but God called me to complete my bachelor's degree. Many times I wanted to drop out and move to Africa; I kept thinking about my calling and the lost. Every time the Lord spoke to me to continue my studies, and I obeyed.

In my early twenties, while serving as a missionary in Asia, I heard the Lord clearly say that by the time I was twenty-five I would have my master's degree. Rolland reminded me of this promise from the Lord and asked me if I thought the degree would simply come in the mail. I realized that I had to go through the work of applying and studying for my next degree. It meant leaving Hong Kong and all the people I loved for a season of more preparation.

A few years later while serving in Hong Kong again, I got extraordinarily sick with an immune system disorder and was not able to read or concentrate. As I was praying in this seriously sick condition, the Lord spoke to me that it was time to go and earn my PhD! I was in shock once again. How could I earn a PhD when I was in such terrible health? How could I leave Asia where there was so much fruit? I knew in the end I would simply obey. I felt called to go to King's College at the University of London and study systematic theology. Four years later I defended my thesis with an external examiner, the Rev. Dr. Martin Percy from Oxford, and graduated.

The point is, if I hadn't obeyed the Lord when I was sixteen, I would not have been able to receive my next promise. Now, as we build the university, I clearly see why God led me to get my PhD. Sometimes we do not understand the direction He takes us in, but He is always trustworthy and always faithful. What incredible fruit awaits us on the other side of our obedience!

During our Global Team meetings it was a joy and a privilege to hear the testimonies of laid-down lovers around the world who worship Papa God with all their hearts and give their lives away to bring Jesus the reward of His suffering—His lost bride around the world. They continuously pour themselves out, as we do, to advance the kingdom of God and invite people into this glorious life of love. They have seen God birth so many miraculous promises in their lives, and they are still waiting, laboring, and believing for many promises not yet seen.

Just as Rolland and I know that together with our team, God has given us the nation of Mozambique, our dear friends Brian and Pamela Jourden know that the Lord has a great revival to birth in Zimbabwe and across Africa. Many prophetic words have been released over their lives, and financial miracles grow their ministry. When they started Generation Won/Iris Zimbabwe in 2008, Zimbabwe had gone from being one of the most prosperous nations in Africa, called the "breadbasket of Africa," to being the poorest nation in the world. God spoke to them that Zimbabwe, which means house of stones, was like the stone the builders rejected, Jesus, but it would become a cornerstone nation, just as Jesus is the chief cornerstone, and a house of prayer for all nations. They have over twenty churches among three tribes, and they have seen HIV/AIDS and cancer miraculously healed as they preach the gospel. God is also opening doors with national leaders.

Though they have already seen mighty things, the

Jourdens also battle against the hostile climate of their nation. The government is very suspicious of foreigners working among the poor, which results in dangerous situations for their ministry. They and their local leaders have been threatened and taken in and interrogated by the police. In a painful but God-led decision, the Jourdens recently left Zimbabwe for the safety of everyone involved in the ministry.

As Brian shared with us at the Global Team meetings, our hearts broke with his over his faithful pastors who continue to lay their lives on the line for the gospel. It was a difficult but necessary decision to leave Zimbabwe at this time, but even in the midst of that they know with all their hearts that they will return and see the Lord's mighty victory. In this season when they had to lay their prophetic promises back at Jesus's feet, they see Him birthing new dimensions to their promises in other nations. They see a transnational revival rising up. The word they hear is that their disappointment can be God's appointment. Even the failures can be stepping-stones to God's greatest triumphs and can catapult us into even greater destiny.

We are so proud of them, and we believe with them for Zimbabwe. Sometimes, like Abraham, we have to lay our dreams down and see what the Lord will do. Our Congolese brothers have suffered in unimaginable ways. Even their trip to Cabo Delgado, where the meeting was held, took about ten days with many roadblocks—they were denied entry at the border, questioned for hours, held up with guns, and their passports were confiscated. They still pressed on in the journey knowing that God wanted them to come.

Also at the meeting we heard from pastor Euclide

Mugisho. He and his wife have had three miscarriages. Their fourth baby was born prematurely and then tragically died along with five other babies when the hospital incubator room overheated. His wife is now seven months pregnant, and as we prayed in faith with our children, we all declared that this baby would be carried to full term.

It was so special to be with our Iris family, hear the amazing things that God is doing, and cheer one another on. In the hard moments we need one another even more, and we believe together that we will see every promise fulfilled.

When I asked the Lord for a message to share with our Iris family, He led me to Philippians. Paul's prayer for the body of Christ was "that your love may abound more and more in knowledge and depth of insight, so that you may be able to discern what is best and may be pure and blameless until the day of Christ, filled with the fruit of righteousness that comes through Jesus Christ—to the glory and praise of God" (Phil. 1:9).

How do we discern what is best? He tells us in the secret place. Beloved, Jesus never makes you tired. He never burns us out. He longs for us to burn continuously with fiery passion and love for Him and for the lost. If you feel tired and burned out, run to the secret place. Even if you feel joyful and ready to take on whatever may come, don't forget to dwell in the secret place and receive Daddy God's plans for each day.

God also gave me a prophetic picture. I saw a chicken and an eagle. The chicken was running around in circles in the dirt. He flapped and flapped and ran in circles, but a chicken simply cannot fly. The strangest thing about chickens is that even if their heads are cut off, they don't know they're dead. They just keep flapping and running in circles. Sometimes we can get so caught up in the needs around us that we don't even notice we are dead and have been separated from our head, Christ Jesus.

In the prophetic picture I also saw an eagle. An eagle soars! He barely needs to flap his wings because he is carried on the wind and sees with heavenly perspective. Our service to God can be the same way. As Isaiah 40:31 says, "Those who hope in the LORD will renew their strength. They will soar on wings like eagles; they will run and not grow weary, they will walk and not be faint."

I pray that each of you will be like eagles. I long for you to be so connected to Jesus that you will never burn out or give up. I also want you to know that Jesus is not nearly as concerned about what you do as He is about how you do it. Do you carry His love, mercy, and kindness? Do people see who Jesus is when they look at you and work with you? I am cheering you on and praying for you to be more like Him every single day. This is my prayer for you:

> *Holy Spirit, overshadow Your sons and Your daughters!*
>
> *Take them deep into the rivers of Your love. Put Your promises within them. Give them Your eyes to see and Your heart to feel. Let them be Your hands extended to love the poor and the broken. Let their feet follow You into the darkest places of the earth without fear, carrying the light of Your glory.*
>
> *May they carry each and every one of Your promises over their lives to full term. Let their joy and strength be sustained forever by the*

rhythm of Your heart. May they know when to rest, when to run, and when to release. May they never give up. May they never fear inconvenience, pain, or the ridicule of men.

Release Your glory on the earth, Father God. Put courage within Your people. Let Your love be made manifest today and every day, for the rest of our lives. Release Your glory so that every lost son and daughter may come home.

Amen.

Contact Information

US office and support address:

Iris Global
PO Box 493995
Redding, CA 96049-3995
USA

Website and online donations: www.irisglobal.org

Email: info@irisglobal.org

Phone: +1-530-255-2077

FOR anyone wondering if authentic community is possible in today's world...

FOR anyone wondering if the Beatitudes still mean something...

FOR anyone wondering how to follow Jesus all the way...

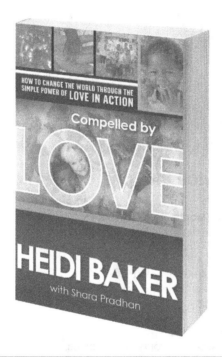

CPSIA information can be obtained
at www.ICGtesting.com
Printed in the USA
LVHW021727230920
666904LV00012B/1017